Revision Guide to AS Level Economics and Business

Alan Hewison

Edited by: **Nancy Wall**

informe

Alan Hewison is an experienced enthusiast for the joint subject approach. He is Head of Economics, Business and Politics at Queen Elizabeth Grammar School, Penrith, Cumbria. He is Principal Examiner for Edexcel's GCE Economics and Business and was part of the team responsible for creating the new specification, particularly Units 2b and 4b. He has been examining for Edexcel (and before that, AQA) for many years.

Nancy Wall was a teacher for the first half of her career. Since 1991 she has worked in curriculum development, with a particular interest in teaching strategies and classroom resource development. She is currently reviews editor of 'Teaching Business and Economics', the magazine of the Economics, Business and Enterprise Association. She has long experience of writing and editing resources for students.

© Anforme Ltd 2011
ISBN 978-1-905504-64-0
Anforme Ltd, Stocksfield Hall, Stocksfield, Northumberland NE43 7TN.
Typeset by George Wishart & Associates, Whitley Bay.
Printed by Potts Print (UK) Ltd.

Contents

Using this book

This book provides revision notes for both of your GCE AS units in Economics and Business (8EB01). For each unit the guide follows the order of the Edexcel specification. There are some sections headed 'Try this' that contain some brief revision exercises. Some suggested answers can be found at the rear of the guide.

This guide should be used in conjunction with your textbook(s) and your class notes – Good Luck!

Exam hints

Look for the 'command' words, they come at the start of the question and give you an idea of what skills you need to use. The important ones to remember are...

- **Explain** – tell the examiner what you know about something.
- **Analyse** – tell the examiner what is likely to happen as a result of something.
- **Assess** or **Evaluate** – tell the examiner what the advantages and disadvantages of something are, then draw a conclusion and support it with appropriate argument.

Finally don't forget to use **context**. This is all about your relating your answer to the specific settings of the question. Answers that are textbook perfect but could be about *any* business or situation, lack context and will not reach the higher levels of the mark scheme.

Assessment of Unit 1: Developing new business ideas – Examination of 1 hour 15 minutes

Section A: 8 supported multiple choice questions worth 4 marks each.   *Total 32 marks*

Section B: questions based on written stimulus material.   *Total 38 marks*

Total 70 marks

Assessment of Unit 2b: Business economics – Examination of 1 hour 15 minutes

Section A: 6 supported multiple choice questions worth 4 marks each.   *Total 24 marks*

Section B: questions based on written stimulus material.   *Total 46 marks*

Total 70 marks

Supported Multiple Choice Questions (SMQs)

- Try and pick the right answer!
- Do your best to say why this is the right answer.
- Be clear in explaining any terms and concepts involved and relate them to the context of the question.
- If you have space, explain why at least one or more of the others is wrong.
- If you don't know the right answer, use a process of elimination; saying why some of the other responses are wrong will still get you some of the marks.

Data questions

- Read the evidence carefully.
- Look for the 'command' words.
- Try to use the proper terms and concepts.
- Use the context of the question in your answer.
- If it says assess or evaluate, make sure that you do! Too many candidates throw marks away each year by not doing this.

Characteristics of successful entrepreneurs

An **entrepreneur** can be briefly defined as someone who organises a business venture and is responsible for the risks involved. The entrepreneur will decide what will be produced and how it will be created, obtain the finance to cover start-up costs and decide the price at which it will be marketed.

Entrepreneurs

Entrepreneurs are responsible for putting business ideas into practice. They must plan the venture, organise the resources needed and then oversee production. Famous examples include Philip Green, Anita Roddick and Richard Branson. Most entrepreneurs are not as high profile or as well known, in fact the great majority run small businesses. The plumber who comes to mend your leaking pipe may be just as much of an entrepreneur as Alan Sugar.

To be successful, the entrepreneur will have to embody a whole range of essential qualities:

Hard work – Without hard work an entrepreneur is unlikely to succeed. This usually means more than the usual 9 to 5 hours, especially in the early days of the business. Committed entrepreneurs will constantly be thinking about the business and working to improve it.

Motivation – An entrepreneur needs to be well motivated with a strong desire to succeed. There will inevitably be setbacks and problems to solve. Without strong motivation to overcome them, the business may fail.

Risk

Risk-taking – An entrepreneur must be prepared to take risks. Business is all about having the foresight to take calculated risks at the right time, in order to be successful. Would-be entrepreneurs who are too cautious are likely to be left behind. Equally, those who are not alert to the inevitable risks may try to do too much too soon and then find they are losing money.

Initiative – Entrepreneurs do not need to be told what to do. They see and seize upon every opportunity to advance the business using their experience and initiative.

Creativity

Creativity – Entrepreneurs need to be able to come up with good ideas or a fresh way of looking at things in order to create and maintain a competitive advantage.

Resilience – Life as an entrepreneur will not be easy or straightforward. Setbacks and failures are commonplace and the entrepreneur will accept the setbacks, learn from the mistakes and carry on. Self confidence can help entrepreneurs to survive.

Perseverance/commitment – Without 100% commitment to the business it is unlikely to succeed and there will be a constant series of problems to solve. Markets are dynamic and need constant monitoring.

Understanding the market – Good entrepreneurs know their market well. This means having an understanding of their customers' needs and wants, their rivals' likely plans and the direction and future of the market as a whole. Successful entrepreneurs can cope with the competition from rival businesses.

Are entrepreneurs, born or made?

Born

Some people say that entrepreneurs are born not made, that it just comes naturally to some people. There are of course, plenty of examples of entrepreneurs who have all the skills needed to succeed, despite little in the way of formal education or training.

Philip Green left school at 15, Richard Branson, James Caan and Alan Sugar at 16, yet they have all been immensely successful. They all have an instinctive grasp of entre-preneurial skills.

Made

For most entrepreneurs there is little doubt that the skills needed can be acquired. There are many formal academic qualifications in business related subjects, including degrees in business start-ups. The government provides a range of services to support the would-be entrepreneur, including Business Link and the Department of Business, Innovation and Skills.

The National Enterprise Academy backed by Peter Jones from Dragons Den is designed to prepare young people for an entrepreneurial career.

What motivates entrepreneurs?

For many people the answer may be obvious – they will say it is all about making profits and getting rich. This may be true for some entrepreneurs but not for all. People like Philip Green, Richard Branson or Rupert Murdoch have long since passed the getting rich stage; they could have retired to a life of luxury long ago. It is something else that is keeping them going.

Motivation

On a much smaller scale the self-employed plumber or artist is not dreaming of their first million. They are more likely to be looking forward to working independently or the satisfaction of following their artistic leanings. This does not mean that profit is unimportant, rather that there are many other things that motivate entrepreneurs.

Profit

Profit – for many people one of the main reasons for running a business is to make money, to improve their lifestyle and secure a good standard of living for themselves and their families. Profit – the difference between sales revenue and costs – will reward successful entrepreneurs for both the hard work and the risks they have had to live with.

Self-actualisation

Self-actualisation – sometimes being able to achieve a dream or an ambition, however modest, is reward enough for taking on the role and risks of being an entrepreneur.

Creativity – for some entrepreneurs the need to produce or build something is the main motive whether it is an artist or potter, an architect or a builder. The satisfaction of seeing their vision become real is the driving motive.

Satisfaction of making things happen – the ability to get things moving, to create and achieve deals that lead to more business.

Independence – being your own boss is a strong motivating factor for many people, knowing that their decisions and not someone else's will determine the success of the business. The absence of a boss is a real attraction for independent-minded people.

Ethical business

Ethical and Green considerations – an increasing number of entrepreneurs want to do the 'right' thing. Their businesses are primarily centred on providing ethical and/or environmentally friendly products. For example, One Water uses its profits to improve supplies of clean water by providing water pumps in African villages.

Social entrepreneurs – A social entrepreneur is someone who uses their entrepreneurial skills to achieve benefits for society. The main aim of social entrepreneurship is to further social and environmental goals. Duncan Goose, who created One Water, would come under this heading. So would Muhammad Yunus, who won the Nobel Peace Prize in 2006 for his founding of the Grameen Bank, which provides credit and banking services to the rural poor.

Leadership styles

Leadership is one of the key skills involved in running a successful business. It has been defined as the art of motivating and organising a group of people to achieve a common goal. The more effectively this can be done the more successful the business will be.

All managers bring their own personal qualities to the task of leadership but there are three broad types of leadership style.

- **Autocratic managers** make all the decisions; they give orders without consulting anyone else. It is a top-down one-way system of communication that can be described as dictatorial.

- **Democratic managers** listen to other people's ideas and opinions before reaching a decision. It is a two-way system of communication, tasks and responsibilities are likely to be delegated.

- **Paternalistic managers**, as the name implies, act as a father might towards their family. They think they know best and although there is some consultation, ultimately the manager takes responsibility and decides what happens. Communication is mostly top-down but with some two-way dialogue. Think David Brent from *The Office*!

	Autocratic	**Paternalistic**	**Democratic**
Consultation	No	Sometimes	Yes
Employees involved in decisions	No	Sometimes	Yes
Delegation	No	Sometimes	Yes
Employees take responsibility	No	Sometimes	Yes
Communication	Top-down, one-way only	Mostly top-down, some two-way	Two-way
Advantages	· Can be useful for guiding new employees · Swift decision making can be crucial in a crisis	· Some consultation · Needs of staff looked after leading to better decisions	· Consultation increases motivation · All ideas considered
Disadvantages	· Useful suggestions from employees not heard · Staff may resent it and become de-motivated	· Still mostly autocratic · Some staff will not like it	· Lengthy decision making · Final decision may be a compromise and not necessarily the 'best' one

Leadership styles

Leadership styles depend a lot on the personality of the entrepreneur or manager.

Which leadership style is best?

Leadership styles depend a lot on the personality of the entrepreneur or the manager. But they also depend on the nature of the business and the traditions within the industry. In the past most leadership styles in manufacturing businesses would have been autocratic. But then Japanese industrialists showed how teamwork could be highly compatible with the achievement of high standards of quality and reliability. (This is sometimes called the **Japanese Way**.) Discussion about how the best outcome might be achieved was encouraged. Leadership styles became more democratic. (See page 80.)

In reality managers will often exhibit some or all of the leadership styles. Think of it as a Venn diagram. The mix of styles adopted by a manager will vary according to the situation. Good managers know which style to use or adapt at any given time to get the best from their staff and the best result for the business.

Figure 1: Overlapping leadership styles

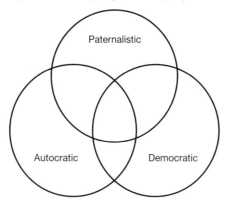

Media businesses often benefit from democratic leadership styles. Creativity is central to their success and having a working atmosphere in which employees are encouraged to contribute their ideas may be vital. But managers may want to be quite autocratic about punctuality and dead-lines, because customer satisfaction often depends on a rigid approach to such things.

Try this

For each leadership style, think of a business that you know about which exemplifies that style. How successful is the business? To what extent has the leadership style affected the way the business works?

McGregor's Theory X and Y

Douglas McGregor was an American social psychologist who proposed his famous X-Y theory in 1960. His idea was that there were two styles of management based on how the managers viewed their workforce. He called these styles Theory X and Theory Y.

Theory X

Theory Y

Theory X managers think that the workforce dislikes work and needs direction and control. Without this and the threat of punishment they will avoid work.

Theory Y managers think the opposite; the workforce is capable of enjoying work and can be trusted to get on with things without close supervision.

Theory X management has much in common with an **autocratic** style of leadership. Theory Y management has much in common with a **democratic** style of leadership. You can probably see a connection between Theory Y and the Japanese Way. The style adopted within the business may well influence the way employees are trained too.

A Theory X style manager assumes that...	A Theory Y style manager assumes that...
• The average person dislikes work	• For the average person work can be as natural as play and rest, and as such, enjoyed
• They will avoid work unless directly supervised	• They can be self motivated and work without supervision
• They must be controlled and directed to ensure that the work is done	• They do not need to be controlled and directed to ensure that the work is done
• The threat of punishment must exist within an organisation	• They respond well to praise and incentives
• People would rather follow others than lead	• People are happy to lead and enjoy responsibility
• People are relatively unambitious and just want security without responsibility	• People are ambitious and will not only accept responsibility but also seek more

Identifying a business opportunity

Markets

What is a market?

> **A market** is any medium in which buyers and sellers interact and agree to trade at a price.

Markets can be real or virtual, small or global. Their key characteristic is that buyers and sellers follow their own interests in a way that determines both the price and quantity traded of a good or service. Wherever someone has something to sell and there is someone who wants to buy that product, a market will spring up. It may be in a particular place, as with a street market, or buyers and sellers may trade without ever seeing each other, using the phone, the internet or eBay. The latter have allowed many new markets to develop.

> **Buyers** are all those people or businesses that want to purchase something. They create the **demand** for goods and services.
>
> **Sellers** are all those people or businesses that want to sell something. They create the **supply** of goods and services.

Demand

> **Demand** – the amount of a good or service that people are willing and able to buy at a given price, at a given time.

Market demand refers to the sum of all individual demands for a particular good or service. (Note that demand has to be *effective*; it is no good just to *want* something. Consumers must be able to pay for it at that price, there and then.)

There is a relationship between price and quantity demanded. This is usually an inverse relationship: as one changes so does the other but in the opposite direction. As **price** (**P**) rises, **quantity** (**Q**) falls and vice versa. You can probably see quite clearly how this works if you like going to the cinema and students are offered cut price tickets with a view to selling more.

When P↑	Q↓
When P↓	Q↑

Demand curve

> A **demand curve** – this relationship can be shown on a diagram called a demand curve. The vertical axis shows the price and the horizontal axis the quantity demanded. The demand curve slopes down from left to right. (Even if it is drawn as a straight line, it will still be called a demand curve.)

Figure 2: The demand curve

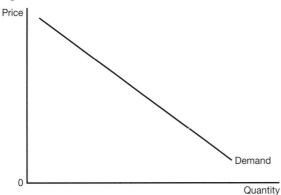

Movement along demand curve

A movement along a demand curve – a change in price

A **change in price** causes a movement **along** the demand curve. This is one way of showing what happens in the case of the cut-price cinema tickets above.

Figure 3: A movement along the demand curve

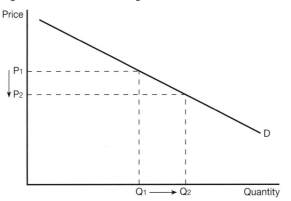

When the price drops from P1 to P2 there is a movement along the demand curve and the quantity demanded increases from Q1 to Q2.

Shift in demand curve

A shift of the demand curve

There are a number of factors that will alter the level of demand at any given price and cause people to buy either more or less of something. This has the effect of shifting the demand curve to the **left** (decrease) or to the **right** (increase). **It is caused by a change in a factor other than price.**

Figure 4: Changes in demand

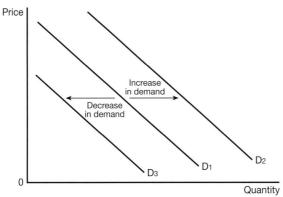

What causes the demand curve to shift?

● **Changes in tastes and fashions** – the consumer's demand for products and services changes all the time, fashions and fads come and go. If the preference for a particular good increases, the demand curve for that good shifts to the right, if it decreases it shifts to the left.

Changes in income

- **Changes in income** – As income changes so too does the quantity demanded. For most goods and services as income rises so too does the quantity demanded and as income drops, so does quantity; these are called **normal goods**. Some goods and services work the other way round, as income increases quantity demanded falls and as income falls demand increases. These are called **inferior goods**. Examples of inferior goods are usually cheaper substitutes, as income fall consumers switch to cheaper products to save money and demand for them increases despite the fall in income. As incomes rise consumers switch back to the more expensive variety.

- **Changes in population** – As population increases or decreases so does the demand for most goods and services. In addition if the structure of the population changes so does demand for certain goods and services, for example a growing number of older people will increase the demand for care homes.

- **Advertising** – The whole point of advertising is to make us all buy more of something i.e. to increase demand and shift the demand curve to the right.

- **Changes in the prices of other goods** – If prices of *related* goods change, the demand curve for the original good can change as well.

Substitutes

1. **Substitutes** are goods that can be consumed in place of one another. If the price of a substitute increases, the demand curve for the original good shifts to the right e.g. if the price of Nescafé increases, the demand for Kenco coffee will increase and the demand curve shifts to the right.

Complements

2. **Complements** are goods that are normally consumed together. If the price of a complement increases, the demand curve for the original good shifts to the left. If the price of a complement decreases, the demand curve for the original good shifts to the right. If, for example, the price of computers falls, then the demand for computer software increases and the demand curve shifts to the right.

> *Try this*
> Think about what happened when people began to download music from the internet. Use the jargon (i.e. terminology) set out above to explain what happened to the demand for CDs, and how this affected the market for music generally.

Supply

> **Supply** – the amount of a good or service that producers are willing and able to supply, at a given price, at a given time.

Market supply

Market supply refers to the sum of all individual suppliers of a particular good or service. (Note that supply has to be *effective*; it is no good just being *willing* to supply something. producers must actually be able to supply it at that price, there and then.)

With supply there is a positive relationship between P and Q. As one changes so does the other but in the same direction. As P rises Q rises and vice versa. Higher prices give suppliers an incentive to produce and sell more.

When P↑	Q↑
When P↓	Q↓

Supply curve

A **supply curve** – this relationship can be shown on a diagram called a supply curve. Like the demand curve the vertical axis shows the price and the horizontal axis the quantity demanded. The supply curve slopes up from left to right. (Even if it is drawn as a straight line, it will still be called a supply curve.)

Figure 5: The supply curve

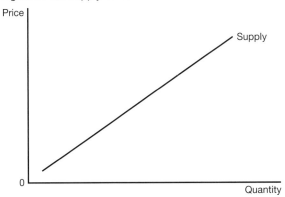

Movement along supply curve

A movement along a supply curve – a change in price

A **change in price** causes a movement **along** the supply curve. Lower prices mean that producers are less inclined to produce for this market; higher prices mean bigger profits and an incentive to produce and sell more.

Figure 6: A movement along the supply curve

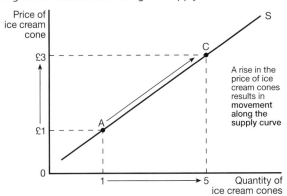

When the prices rises from £1 to £3 there is a movement along the supply curve and the quantity supplied increases from 1 to 5.

Shift in supply curve

A shift of the supply curve

There are a number of factors that will alter the level of supply at any given price and cause people to buy either more or less of something. This has the effect of shifting the supply curve to the **left** (decrease) or to the **right** (increase). It is caused by a change in a factor **other than price**.

Figure 7: A shift in the supply curve

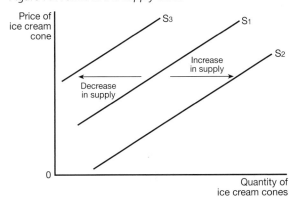

Causes of supply curve shifts

- **Change in costs** – An increase in costs shifts the supply curve to the left. If a furniture maker has to pay more for wood, then profits decline. The less attractive profit opportunities may mean the producer cuts output, shifting the supply curve of furniture to the left. If costs decline, firms respond by increasing output. The furniture manufacturer may increase production if wood costs fall. Technical changes are a very important reason why costs may fall.

- **Change in size of the industry** – If the size of an industry grows, the supply curve shifts to the right. The fast-food industry, for example, exploded in the latter half of the twentieth century as more and more fast food chains entered the market. The supply curve shifts to the left as the size of an industry shrinks. For example, the supply of manual typewriters declined dramatically in the 1990s as the number of producers dwindled.

- **Imposition of a tax** – When the government intervenes in a market it may be because it wants to tax a product to cut consumption or raise revenue (as with petrol). An increase in the tax on a product shifts the supply curve to the left. In effect the costs for the producer have increased by the amount of the tax.

- **Natural phenomena** – The supply of some goods is dependent on events beyond the producer's control e.g. the supply of wheat depends on the quality of the harvest, a poor harvest will send the supply curve to the left. Some goods are dependent on the existence of natural resources e.g. the discovery of new oilfields will shift the supply curve for oil to the right.

- **New technologies** – a technology change shifts the supply curve to the right. Technological progress allows firms to produce a given item at a lower cost. Computer prices, for example, have declined radically as technology has improved, lowering their cost of production.

➡ How to get the demand and supply curves the right way round

Every year some exam candidates get their curves mixed up. Remember them this way…

Demand starts with a **D** – the demand curve slopes **D**own from L to R

Supply has the word **UP** in it – the supply curve slopes **UP** from L to R

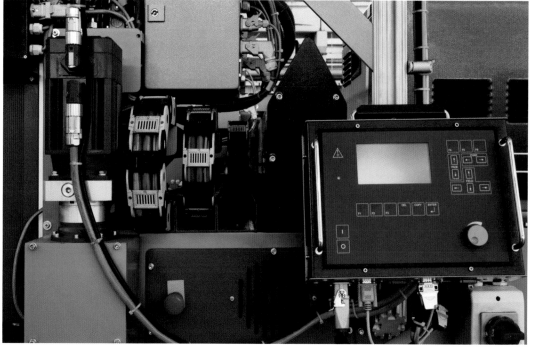

Investment in better equipment cuts costs.

The interaction of demand and supply

Equilibrium price

- When the demand and supply curves are brought together on the same diagram there is a point at which the curves cross each other.

- This is the **equilibrium point**. At this point, the quantity demanded is the same as the quantity supplied. At the equilibrium price there will be no unsold stocks and customers will be able to buy all they demand at that price.

- It is the price and quantity set by market forces.

- Supply and demand together determine the prices of the economy's goods and services.

- In market economies, prices are the signals that guide the **allocation of resources**. They indicate clearly to suppliers when consumers want more or less of their product.

Figure 8: Equilibrium price and quantity

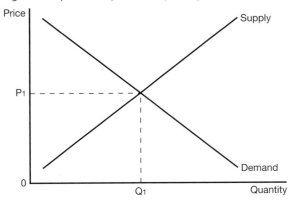

Market forces

The implications of **market forces** for businesses are very important. Rising prices may indicate increasing demand. Business managers who understand their market may realise that they can safely increase output and perhaps also raise prices, so increasing their profits substantially. On the other hand demand may be falling and orders diminishing. A price cut may arrest the slide but more likely, the business will need to cut output before it starts to make significant losses. To stay alive it may have to come up with a new and more popular product.

The business that can come up with a new product or devise a new way to make an existing product more cheaply will be able to cut costs and prices. This will lead to consumers demanding larger quantities and perhaps to the business getting a larger share of the market.

Successful businesses are sensitive to changes in market forces and their likely implications. Success may mean expansion and growth, but businesses can also succeed without growing. If they can make enough profit to give their owners and employees a living and in the long run, cover the cost of the capital equipment they need to function, they will survive. Many people in business would regard this as success, even if it never becomes spectacular.

Usually the key to success is market orientation. This is particularly important in markets which are very competitive, where consumers have many products to choose from and it is quite hard to make a profit.

Market orientation

Market orientation is achieved when a business focuses its activities, products and services around the wants and needs of the customer. The result is that the business adapts its products or innovates to give the customers what they want and compete successfully with rival suppliers.

By contrast, the business that is product orientated has its primary focus on the product – and on the skills, knowledge and systems that support that product. This may help to ensure product quality but if it is not exactly what the customers want, sales may be disappointing.

Market orientation

Benefits of market orientation

- By focusing on the wants and needs of the customer the business is much more likely to produce a product or service that the customer wants and will therefore buy.

- This will give that business a **competitive advantage** over rival businesses, which may not be so closely focused on the customer.

- If the customer is kept satisfied by the business then **brand loyalty** may be created and the customer is more likely to purchase more products or services from the business.

- A satisfied customer is likely to recommend the business to friends and family.

- Increasing brand loyalty means that it may be easier for the business to charge a higher price for its products and services.

During the recession in 2009, the US car giant, Ford, faced rapidly falling sales. Rising unemployment meant that incomes were falling generally. But that was not all. Many potential buyers had decided to buy the smaller, more economical cars produced in the Far East. Many of them didn't want Ford's gas guzzlers any more. The US government stepped in with loans to help Ford, but only on condition that it shut down some of its old production facilities and redesigned its products.

Try this
Explain what was happening in the market for cars, using the ideas relating to demand and supply above. Explain what Ford had to do to rescue its situation. Would you describe Ford as product or market orientated?

Evaluating a business opportunity

Market research

> **Market research** is any kind of activity that gives a business information about its product or service, its customers, its competitors or the market it operates in.

Why do businesses need market research?
- To identify what's happening in the market **now**.
- To predict what might happen in the market **in the future**.
- To explore **new** possibilities in the market.

Market research...
- ...gives information that can be used to make better informed decisions about the business and its future.
- ...allows businesses to understand consumer behaviour, to make decisions that make them more responsive to customers' needs and to increase profits.
- ...helps to give a business a **competitive advantage** by improving its products and/or services and successfully marketing them.
- ...is crucial for any business start up, to reduce the risks involved.
- ...is also essential for established businesses to keep up with market trends and remain competitive.

The information gathered can be in many different forms and of many different types. Market research falls into two main categories, **Primary** and **Secondary Research**.

> **Primary Research** – The gathering of information first hand from an original source, that has not been collected before. Often involves going out and asking people for specific information hence its alternative name **Field Research**. Examples include questionnaires, focus groups and direct interviews. Direct observation may be important too, especially for small businesses, and may help in deciding where to locate.

> **Secondary Research** – Finding and using information that has already been gathered by somebody else. Sometimes called **Desk Research**, as it can be done by reading books and journals, or using online information. Examples include Google, trade journals and National Statistics.

Market research will be rather different for business start-ups, compared to what may happen in a long-established business. A new business may be looking initially for a small, local market. There may be a gap in the local shopping centre, a need that is not catered for by the existing retailers. Maybe there is no health food shop, or no antique or junk shop. This may mean there is a profitable market. Equally, some places have many antique and junk shops. That may be a place that collectors visit purposely to get a good choice of second-hand stuff. In that case, another shop could well be profitable, despite the competition. Close observation of local markets is sometimes the key to a successful start-up.

Usually observation of this kind will have to be backed up by other kinds of primary research. Interviews may be helpful. Secondary research could include analysis of local population trends. There might be no retail outlet for baby clothes and equipment but if the area has a high concentration of elderly people, this may not be profitable. www.neighbourhood.statistics.gov.uk has useful data that provides information on local trends.

Long-established businesses can put extensive resources into researching the market for a new product. They may be looking for gaps in a wider market so researching customer preferences becomes very important. You might think that yoghurt comes in so many different forms that finding a new, distinctive product might be difficult. But within the live, fat-free category there were relatively few choices. Onken came up with a fat free live strawberry yoghurt that was on its own, at least for a while. That would have been preceded by conducting focus group discussions with people who bought live fat free yoghurt. For all businesses, market research can reduce risks. The choice of research techniques will depend on the product and the location.

	Primary research	Secondary research
Advantages	• Can be designed specifically to suit the purpose of the business • Information will be up to date and directly relevant • Information gathered is not available to competitors.	• Can be done very quickly, particularly online • Can be much cheaper than primary research.
Disadvantages	• Can be expensive to collect, particularly if employing an agency • Can take a long time • Can give misleading information if questions not worded correctly or there are errors in sampling.	• May not be exactly specific to researcher's needs • Can be dated • May not be accurate, particularly if an online source.

Quantitative and qualitative research

Quantitative research

Qualitative research

Quantitative research is based on numerical data, measures things and produces statistical information e.g. the number of times 18 to 25 year olds go to the cinema or the percentage of Toyota's sales now made in China. The main types of quantitative research are sampling and questionnaires.

Qualitative research is based on consumer's attitudes and opinions. It tries to identify why consumers behave the way they do e.g. how they react to a new product, how does the customer feel when buying chocolate. The main types of qualitative research are focus groups and interviews.

Quantitative research produces data on market size and buyers' other characteristics such as age, gender and location. Qualitative research goes much deeper and produces information about how customers feel about the product. In both cases, strategies for gathering information are changing. There are far fewer face-to-face interviews than there used to be, as researchers use the telephone or the internet to gather information. Supermarkets keep in close touch with customers using their loyalty cards. These approaches cut the cost of market research. However, many businesses still attach great weight to designers' judgement about what is likely to succeed. The best example of this approach is Apple, which has repeatedly developed new and very successful products, based on creativity and innovation.

Sampling

> **Sampling** – It would be practically impossible to interview everybody in a particular market and so a smaller section or sample of the market is chosen as being representative of the whole.

If it is to be useful and accurate, the sample must be representative of the whole of the target market and not be biased in any way. It is important to choose a sample that is appropriate for that particular task. As a general rule, the larger the sample, the more accurate it is likely to be in estimating the characteristics of the market. Small samples are likely to be biased towards one particular part of the market, and may therefore produce biased results.

Sampling methods

Random sample

Stratified sample

Quota sample

> **Random sample** – a group of people selected so as to be representative of the population as a whole. Interviewing people as they happen to walk by will result in a biased sample. The composition of the group will change according to the location and the time of day, and may include few people who have jobs. Appropriate methods might be to pick addresses at random from the electoral register or numbers chosen from the phone book.
>
> **Stratified sampling** – This involves targeting one particular segment of the market that you want to find out about. A maker of baby foods might only interview mothers between the ages of 16 and 30.
>
> **Quota sampling** – This means segmenting the market into groups that share specific characteristics. The research then focuses on a specific number (quota) of each group. For example, out of 100 interviewees 50% should be men, of that 50%, 10 % should be below 20 years old, another 10% aged between 20 and 30 and so on.

	Advantages	Disadvantages
Random sampling	● Can be effective and accurate	● Hard to be truly random in practice ● Needs large sample sizes to be accurate ● Can be expensive
Stratified sampling	● Targets market effectively	● Difficulty in identifying appropriate strata ● More complex to organise and analyse results.
Quota sampling	● Cheap and effective way of sampling.	● Need to be careful in drawing up quotas to avoid bias.

Markets

Markets vary hugely. They will be affected by all the things that have an impact on demand and supply – the subject of Section 1.3.2 (pages 6-11). Many small businesses are looking for local markets. But some small businesses produce highly specialised products and sell them all over the world. Bigger businesses typically have fewer competitors and become very preoccupied with their market shares – as with supermarket chains.

Market size is normally measured by the total sales of all the businesses in that market added together.

Market share of an individual business can be expressed by total sales (£) as a percentage of the overall market. For example, in October 2010 the UK clothing market was estimated to be worth £25.2 billion, Primark had a 10.2% share of the market, or £2.57 billion.

Market share

Market growth

- **Market growth** is an increase in the demand for a product. It can be rapid if the product is new and many people want it or it can be slow or static if the product is well established. A negative growth rate would mean that the product is facing falling demand.

- A **mass market** is, as its name implies, a very large market with a high value of sales by volume. Mass marketing occurs when one product is aimed at the largest group of consumers for a particular product or service, e.g. washing up liquid.

- A **niche market** is a small part of an overall market that has certain special characteristics, these may include providing a specialised or luxury product or service, having little competition and being able to charge a higher price. For example some consumers will only buy eco-friendly washing up liquid.

Generally speaking, smaller markets will tend to be less competitive. In a niche market it may be easier to survive if there are fewer competing businesses. The potential profit may be too small to attract big businesses.

Many businesses in niche markets have been helped along by internet sales. If they can reach people with very individual needs electronically, they can locate wherever they find convenient and still have access to interested customers anywhere.

Try this

Identify a business with a niche market and consider how successful it is. What are the key factors on which its success depends, and why?

The scope for market growth depends on a whole range of factors. For luxury products, richer people need to be gaining ground with rising incomes. Sometimes products that offer very good value do well when incomes are falling. When recession started to bite in the UK in 2009, many people decided not to go on holiday, so day trips to Brighton increased. (Luxury products are generally normal goods, while days out in Brighton are inferior goods, see page 8.)

Fashions can play a part, and new technologies can mean expanding markets for new products and shrinking markets for old ones. A new product may be a good substitute for an older one – so the latter may face falling sales and some businesses may close down production.

Market segmentation

**Market
segments**

> **Market segmentation** means dividing the market into groups of consumers with similar characteristics. Common groupings include; age, gender, income, interests, location etc. This enables products and services to be more effectively produced and targeted for a particular segment.

A market contains many different types of customer; it is unlikely that one product will satisfy all consumers in the market. For example one magazine is unlikely to appeal to both sexes old and young. Markets are therefore split up into groups of consumers that have similar wants and needs. Alternatively, markets may be segmented by product. For example, buyers of 4-wheel drive vehicles constitute one segment of the car market. Or a market may be segmented according to the level of luxury involved, as with clothing.

Catering for the needs of small market segments may raise costs and prices. Standardised products with a mass market cost less to produce. But if customers value the products that are designed to suit them the best, they will be prepared to pay a bit more to get exactly what they want.

● Some segments are very large and general, e.g. The Radio Times is just aimed at anyone who watches television whereas Vintage Tractors magazine is clearly aimed at a small group of people with a common interest in the subject.

● There are many ways of segmenting the market; these are just some of them:
 · Socio-economic grouping
 · Income, age and gender
 · Size and composition of customer households
 · Geographical location
 · Ethnicity and/or religion
 · Educational background of customers
 · Hobbies and interests

Advantages of segmentation	Disadvantages of segmentation
● The more precisely a segment can be identified and provided for, the more likely it is that a sale will be made	● Can be expensive to research and identify different segments
● Segmenting the market reduces direct competition	● More costly to develop and market different products for different segments rather than just one standardized product
● A premium price may be charged if market segments get exactly what they want	● Targeting one particular segment may mean ignoring others
● Encourages the development of brand loyalty	● Even if segments are identified, reaching them may be another problem

Market positioning

**Market
position**

> **Market positioning** is how individual products or brands are seen in relation to their competition by the consumers. This may involve a number of changes in price or quality.
>
> **Product differentiation** occurs when businesses make their product a little different from competing products. This may involve giving it unique features which may attract customers, or it may involve changing perceptions as to the function of the product.

Product differentiation

Market positioning concerns how the business places its products in relation to competing products in the minds of consumers. Businesses need to decide if they want to follow the competition with a similar product or whether they want to create a 'different' image for their product. A business that has found a gap in the market will differentiate its product so as to fill that gap.

Positioning the product in the right place can be very beneficial. It may be best to be close to the market leader, e.g. the new generation of phones mimicking the iPhone. Or it may be possible to go to a part of the market that is yet to be catered for, as Dyson did with the original bagless vacuum cleaners. A distinctive product is more likely to secure some degree of customer loyalty.

Repositioning

Businesses with long-existing products may decide to re-position them in the market. In the 1990s, the image of Skoda cars was so poor that they were the subject of jokes. Skoda retained its market position in the minds of customers as a very competitively priced car, but successfully re-positioned itself by improving reliability and so becoming an award winning car manufacturer. Customer perceptions shifted to regard the cars as generally better value for money.

In some cases businesses have re-positioned themselves from one segment to another. The best example is Lucozade, which moved from being a health drink to aid recovery from illness, to a best-selling, trendy sports drink for athletes! There was no change in the product but advertising subtly changed customer perceptions about its possible uses.

Market mapping

Market map

> **Market mapping** is the use of a grid showing two features of a market, such as price and consumer age. Individual brands or businesses are added to the grid to show potential niches or gaps in the market. It also helps to position products in relation to each other.

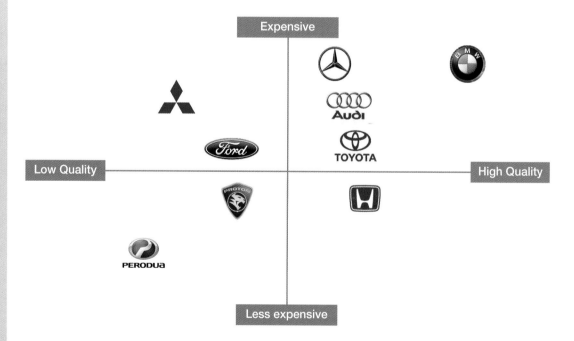

In this market map the grid shows quality and price as the determining characteristics. Some car manufacturers are plotted onto it. There appears to be a gap for a maker of quality but less expensive cars on the lower right side. Arguably Skoda has repositioned their brand here.

Advantages of market mapping	Disadvantages of market mapping
• Enables a business to spot gaps in the market	• Can be hard to categorise some products and services
• Can help a business to differentiate its product from the competition	• Identifying a gap does not mean there is a need for a product to fill it. More research must be done

Competitive advantage

Competitive advantage

Competitive advantage is any feature of a business that enables it to compete effectively with rival products. An advantage may be based on price, quality, service, reputation or innovation. A convenient location may be significant. Product differentiation may be used to achieve an advantage.

Adding value means altering the product so as to increase its value to the customer. All businesses add value to the product either by improving it in some way or by providing it in the locations where customers want it.

In competitive markets, all businesses must strive for competitive advantage in order to avoid falling sales and rising losses. Cutting costs can allow a business to compete on price. Investment in new production technologies or improving relationships with suppliers may cut costs. New technologies can also create opportunities to improve product design or introduce completely new products. Improvements in staff training may lead to improved product reliability or customer service.

Adding value

Businesses that enhance their competitive advantages by cutting prices or **adding value** to the product are likely to be able to sell more and sometimes raise prices too. It helps to reduce competition if consumers see something a little different about the product or service:

Better staff training might improve hotel service.

- Perceived good value for money may be based on a low price or a reputation for quality.

- A brand image may become associated with technical excellence or appealing design features.

- Competitive advantage applies to services as well as manufactures. It is easy to see how better staff training might improve the services offered in a hotel or a fitness centre.

Try this
Explain how these businesses maintain their competitive advantage: John Lewis, Apple, Boeing, Vauxhall, Premier Inns and your local convenience store.

Product trial

Test marketing

A **product trial** or **test marketing** consists of launching the product on a limited scale in a representative segment of the market to measure initial reactions.

- This will show whether the product is viable before rolling it out to the rest of the market.

- This avoids the costs of a full-scale launch as well as providing useful market data which may then be used, if necessary, to adapt or modify the product.

- For example: Coca-Cola test-marketed a new carbonated drink at natural food stores and delis in New York, under the name Vio. If it succeeded in the United States they planned to launch it globally.

- Test marketing is expensive, even though it is cheaper than a nationwide product launch. It involves setting up production processes for a product that may or may not turn out to be successful, and it may provide competing businesses with advance information about a new product.

Test marketing is particularly useful to food manufacturers, for whom there is always a possibility that a new product will not match up with customer tastes. It could save them from an expensive flop. But the high costs involved mean that it will usually be used cautiously. A key question in any product trial is whether customers will come back for repeat purchases. A market in which customers want to buy the product just once will shrink rapidly after the initial launch period is over.

Opportunity cost

Opportunity cost

Opportunity cost is the cost of the next best alternative that has been sacrificed. Resources are scarce and choices have to be made. Every spending decision has an opportunity cost, which is what we have foregone to get the product in question.

Everyone has to make choices in life and opportunity cost is a key consideration when making spending decisions.

- You may have to decide what to do with your time, whether to stay in and study or go out to meet friends.

- A business may have to decide which investment project to choose, perhaps a new computer system or a new delivery van.

- Governments have to choose between spending on schools and other things, perhaps healthcare or roads.

Scarcity and choice

The same concept applies in each case. Because, ultimately, resources are **scarce**, consumers, businesses and governments must decide which of the possible alternatives are most desirable. **Choices** must be made because individuals, businesses and governments never have all the funds they would need to buy everything they want.

Once the choice has been made, the alternative has been sacrificed and that will be the opportunity cost. If you stay in and study you have sacrificed (given up) the opportunity to go out. The opportunity cost is not meeting your friends. If the business chooses the new van it can no longer afford the computer system. The opportunity cost of the van is the computer system. The idea of opportunity cost is particularly useful in situations where the ultimate benefits of the spending decision may be uncertain.

When a business start-up is being planned, and also when an established business is planning new product developments, there will be opportunity costs to consider. Going for one particular product means that it will not be possible also to develop an alternative. The opportunity cost of one product will be the potential profit foregone by not going ahead with a different product. It will usually be possible to identify a range of possible business activities, only one of which can be actively pursued. So exploring the relative profitability of several different ideas will be important in the planning process. Alongside this, the business will consider the enthusiasm and commitment that the owners, the managers and key employees can bring to the development process. This may be strong enough to make the opportunity cost of alternatives seem quite low, even if they are potentially profitable.

Trade-offs

Opportunity costs and trade-offs

> A **trade-off** is a situation where having more of one thing leads to having less of another. It is linked to the concept of opportunity cost.

We often think about opportunity cost in an either/or situation, where we must choose one thing over another. A trade-off involves a more gradual lessening of one variable in order to get more of another.

For example if you face a straightforward choice between staying in on a Friday night or going out, your decision will involve opportunity cost. If you stay in the opportunity cost is not going out. However if you look at this choice throughout the year there is a trade-off between the time you spend studying to get a good grade and the total time spent socialising. More time spent going out means less time with your books and perhaps not as good a grade!

- Businesses face trade-offs all the time as well, there is for example, a trade-off between money spent on developing new products and money spent promoting existing ones. The business will have a certain level of finance available for promotion and more of one will mean less of the other. Within the business, different departments will try to calculate the costs and benefits of promotional activity in order to argue their respective cases to senior managers. Market researchers will need to estimate likely future sales revenue, using all the information they can get.

- When contemplating a business start-up, there may be a significant trade-off to be considered because the work involved may mean losing time spent with family or on recreational activities. Being self employed often means having to work longer hours than an employer would require.

Stakeholders

> **Stakeholders** are individuals or groups with an interest in the actions of a business. Stakeholders include: employees, owners & shareholders, customers, suppliers, the local community, competitors and the government.

Stakeholders will all have an interest in the actions of a business but they will not necessarily all want the same outcome.

Shareholders

For example owners and shareholders will want the maximum profits from the business while employees will want higher wages and customers want lower prices. If a business expands this may be good for the employees and owners but not so good for the local community, which may have to put up with increased traffic and pollution. This is called stakeholder conflict. In fact there is a trade-off between the needs and wants of different stakeholder groups.

The significance of stakeholder interests is much debated in the business world. Broadly, there are three views:

Profitability

- In managing a business, the overriding objective is to follow the interests of the shareholders. They are the owners of the business and their primary interest is in profitability. (This may be a long term or a short term interest.) Market forces will ensure that other stakeholders derive benefits from the operations of the business.

Employees

- All stakeholder interests should be taken into account when business decisions are taken. All stakeholders have valid points of view and responsible businesses will consider these. This is a standpoint that has ethical and moral aspects. In the nineteenth century, some businesses built housing for their employees, for example the Cadburys village at Bourneville. This was at a time when, typically, employers paid their workers the lowest wage consistent with being able to recruit them and many lived in overcrowded and unsanitary conditions. More recently, some businesses have worked hard to reduce the environmental damage caused by their activities.

Environmental issues

- A third view sees attention to stakeholder interests as an important factor in ensuring the long-term success of the business. This way, the business can expect more support from both the community and the government, perhaps both locally and nationally. It may be able to improve motivation and lower staff turnover by paying higher wages. In short, taking stakeholder interests into account will be good for profits in the long run.

You don't have to be a genius to see that the Deepwater Horizon oil spill in 2010 damaged BP's profits and its reputation very seriously. It and its partner companies apparently kept costs down by neglecting safety precautions, despite being warned by some of their own experts. However, while many people in business might agree that BP's policies were short-sighted, they might also retain the view that shareholders' interests are paramount.

> ### ➡ Stakeholder issues and trade-offs are often complicated
>
> Exam answers often require you to present points of view and show how they relate to specific businesses. This is a great opportunity to construct your argument, back it up with evidence and then explain why another point of view may have some validity.

Economic considerations

All businesses are affected by what goes on in the economy and by the actions of the government. For this section you need to know about unemployment, inflation, exchange rates, interest rates and government changes to the level of taxation and spending. You also need to know the effects they will have on a business.

Current data

Try this

It will be useful to know what the current figures are and whether they are rising or falling. As part of your revision, complete the following table with up to date statistics.

	Figure/percentage	Rising/static/falling
Unemployment – claimant count		
Unemployment – ILO		
Inflation		
Exchange rate £/$		
Exchange rate £/€		
Interest rate		

Unemployment

Unemployment can be defined as the number of people able and willing to work but not able to find a paying job.

Unemployment does **not** include full-time students, the retired, children, or those not actively looking for a paying job.

Rather confusingly there are different ways of calculating the number of unemployed:

Claimant count

- The **claimant count** is the official measure based on the number of people claiming unemployment related benefit.

ILO unemployment

- The **International Labour Organisation** (**ILO**) definition of unemployment is measured through the Labour Force Survey and covers those people who are looking for work and are available for work.

The claimant count is significantly lower than the ILO figure:

- The claimant count for key out-of-work benefits was 1.64 million in October 2010.

- ILO defined unemployment in October 2010 was 2.46 million.

- Big difference!! (820,000 people.)

The level of unemployment has an impact on businesses

Rising unemployment

Unemployment and falling incomes

- As more people become unemployed they have less income and so spend less. Demand for some businesses that sell luxury or non-essential items may fall e.g. foreign holidays, new cars, designer clothes, restaurant meals.

- However some businesses will increase business as people with less money switch to cheaper substitutes. For example, sales of Domino's pizzas saw a 12% increase in turnover as unemployment rose during 2009, as people switched from the more expensive option of eating out to the cheaper take-away pizza option.

- Wages are less likely to increase as there is more competition for the remaining jobs.

- It should be easier to recruit employees as there are more unemployed people to choose from.

- It should be easier to find people with skills that are normally scarce.

Falling unemployment

- As more unemployed people find jobs they now have more income to spend, this should increase demand for most businesses, particularly those that sell luxury or non-essential items e.g. foreign holidays, new cars, designer clothes and restaurant meals.

- Those businesses that sell cheaper substitutes may see a fall in sales as there are now fewer people on restricted incomes.

Rising incomes

- Wages are more likely to increase as employers compete to attract the best people available.

- It may be harder to recruit employees as there are fewer unemployed people to choose from.

- It may be harder to find people with the right skills.

Inflation

Inflation is a sustained increase in the average price level of a country; this is a fall in the value of money.

Measuring inflation

The rate of inflation is measured by the annual percentage change in the level of prices. A sustained fall in the general price level is called deflation – in this situation, the rate of inflation becomes negative.

Rather confusingly there are several measures of inflation. The two main ones are…

- The CPI (Consumer Price Index) is based on the HCIP (Harmonised Consumer index prices) which measures inflation on internationally agreed standards throughout Europe.

- The RPI (Retail price index) includes mortgage interest payments. The RPI also includes council tax.

- The CPI is compiled using a representative selection of more than 600 separate goods and services for which price movements are regularly measured in 146 areas throughout the UK.

- Some 130,000 separate price quotations are used each month in compiling the index, which is published each month.

Monetary policy

The government has a 'target' rate of 2% for the level of inflation. The **Bank of England** via the Monetary Policy Committee (MPC) has the responsibility of controlling the rate of inflation. It does this by adjusting the base rate of interest in order to affect interest rates throughout the economy.

Real values

A word about 'real'

Inflation means that the value of money changes over time and it can be confusing to try and make comparisons. Economists use the word real to describe data that take away the effects of inflation and explain what is actually happening. For example, if someone on a salary of £30,000 in 2009 receives a 10% increase to £33,000 in 2010, it does not mean that they are 10% better off in real terms. If inflation has been running at 6% throughout the year, it means that in real terms (what they can actually buy in the form of goods and services) their salary has gone up by just 4%.

Inflation is regarded as one of the most serious problems that can happen to an economy.

The rate of inflation has an impact on businesses

Consequences of inflation

- It is hard to plan for the future when there is uncertainty regarding future costs. This may make businesses less likely to invest.

- Inflation may mean that the costs of supplies and wages are rising. This can reduce profitability unless the business can put its prices up. However higher prices may lead to a fall in quantity demanded.

- Consumers on fixed incomes lose out because their real incomes fall. Some pensions and some kinds of investment income do not rise with inflation.

- Other consumers may not be able to negotiate pay rises to keep up with the rate of inflation; they too have less real income and spend less on goods and services.

- If UK businesses are experiencing a higher rate of inflation than their foreign competitors, it may mean that UK costs are rising faster. In order to maintain profit levels UK firms may put their prices up and lose competitiveness and face falling export sales.

- By the same logic, imports from countries with lower rates of inflation may increase and take sales away from the now more expensive UK businesses.

- The main way to reduce inflation has been to increase interest rates; this increases the cost of borrowing. This affects businesses as they are less likely to invest and grow. Consumers face increased credit charges and mortgage payments. They are less likely to borrow money and spend, which may reduce sales for many businesses.

Interest rates

An **interest rate** can be seen simply as the price of borrowed money. If you want a loan it will eventually have to be repaid with interest. If you borrow £10,000 at an interest rate of 5%, the amount to be repaid at the end of a year will be £10,000 + £500 (5%), i.e. £10,500. Interest rates vary depending on the level of risk involved in the loan.

The higher the interest rate, the more expensive it is to borrow money. Demand theory tells us that the more expensive something is, the less we demand of it. This means that if interest rates generally are increasing, people and businesses will borrow less money. In turn this leads to a reduction in spending and in the overall level of demand in the economy. If this happens there is less demand for goods and services and businesses will slow or cut production. Some businesses will be affected more than others. If interest rates decrease, the opposite will happen.

Interest rate changes

Why do interest rates change?

Interest rates change because all interest rates charged by banks, building societies and other financial institutions are linked to, and heavily influenced by, the base rate of interest set by the Bank of England's Monetary Policy Committee (MPC). Since 1997 the MPC has met once a month to decide whether to increase, maintain or decrease the base rate.

Interest rates increase	Impact on businesses	Impact on consumers
⬆	They are less likely to borrow money to expand. Investment may slow which may lead to fewer new businesses starting up and less growth in existing ones.	They are less likely to borrow money for larger items such as cars and holidays. Spending on credit cards may be reduced. Mortgage repayments will increase leaving less disposable income for other spending. Many businesses will face falling demand.
Interest rates decrease ⬇	Investment may increase and existing businesses may expand. New businesses may be encouraged to start up due to the lower cost of borrowing.	Consumer spending may increase as it is now cheaper to borrow money with loans or credit cards. Mortgage repayments may decrease leaving more disposable income for other spending. Many businesses will experience rising demand.

Exchange rates

Trade and exchange rates

- An exchange rate is the price of one currency expressed in terms of another e.g. £1 = $1.65.

- This means that an American would need to 'pay' $1.65 to 'buy' each £... or, we would need to 'pay' 61p to 'buy' each $.

- Most exchange rates are said to be 'floating', so their price (exchange rate) is determined by the market forces of demand and supply. It behaves just like any good or service. The demand for, and supply of, a currency are created by trade and investment flows.

- In order for trade to take place, currencies have to be exchanged.

- If we sell exports to France they must buy pounds with their euros to pay for them. This increases the demand for pounds.

- If we buy imports from France we have to buy euros with our pounds to pay for them. This increases the supply of pounds.

- Foreign exchange dealers make continuous adjustments to exchange rates, depending upon how much is demanded or supplied of a particular currency.

Exchange rate changes

- Millions of such transactions take place every day so currencies are continually being bought and sold on the foreign exchange markets.
- In case you were wondering that's about $3.2 trillion a day, or $3,200,000,000,000! – which is roughly 16 times more than the annual GDP of the UK!

Depreciation

Exchange rate of the £	What happens...
£ Rises	If the exchange rate of the pound changes from £1 = $1.75 to £1 = $2.00, the pound is said to be 'stronger' or 'has risen'. The correct term is '**appreciation**'. Each pound can now buy **more** dollars than it did before
£ Falls	If the exchange rate of the pound changes from £1 = $1.75 to £1 = $1.50, the pound is said to be 'weaker' or 'has fallen'. The correct term is '**depreciation**'. Each pound can now buy **fewer** dollars than it did before

How does this affect a business?

Exchange rates and business decisions

Much will depend upon how much the business is involved with international trade. However, many businesses that don't export can still be affected if some of their inputs are imported.

- Businesses that export will want a depreciating or weaker £ – it will make them more competitive.
- Businesses that import will want an appreciating or stronger £, as their costs will fall and they can reduce prices or make more profit.

Appreciation

Exchange rate of the £	What happens...	Exporters	Importers
The pound appreciates (gets stronger)	Exports become more expensive as foreign countries have to give up more of their money for the same number of pounds Our imports become cheaper as we have to give up fewer pounds to buy the same amount of foreign currency	 **Unhappy!**	 **Happy!**
The pound depreciates (gets weaker)	Exports become cheaper as foreign countries have to give up less of their money for the same number of pounds Our imports become more expensive as we have to give up more pounds to buy the same amount of foreign currency	 **Happy!**	 **Unhappy!**

An easy way to remember all this...

SPICED

Strong Pound Imports Cheap Exports Dear

(The other way round is WPIDEC – which isn't as easy to remember!)

Government intervention

Although it is the Bank of England that decides on the base rate and influences monetary policy, it is the government that decides on two other main variables that affect all businesses in the UK. – **government spending** and **levels of taxation**. Both of these affect businesses directly, as well as indirectly through their effects on consumers.

Each year in the Budget, the government sets out its intended level of spending and anticipated income (taxation). By altering the levels of either or both of them, the government can affect the overall level of economic activity and encourage a higher or lower level of consumption and spending.

Government spending

In the year 2009 – 2010 the government planned to spend a total of £669.26bn, this was spread across areas such as education, healthcare, defence, welfare benefits, pensions etc. This expenditure creates income for a vast number of individuals and businesses.

How does it affect business?

Impact of government spending on the economy

- Government employees such as teachers, nurses, civil servants, social workers, armed forces etc. account for just over 6 million people (ONS 2009). All of these will have an income to spend with businesses.

- Many businesses rely on government contracts either to supply equipment and materials to bodies such as schools and the health service, or they build and maintain facilities and infrastructure such as roads and hospitals. They too employ people, who in turn spend money with businesses.

- Many people such as pensioners and the unemployed rely on benefits, the level of which depends on the government.

- If the government cuts/increases its spending, somewhere along the line people and businesses will see a reduction/increase in their income and business activity will be affected.

Taxation

All of this expenditure needs to be paid for and most of this comes from tax revenue (the remainder comes from the borrowing needed to make up the difference). There are many different types of tax but they can be split into two main kinds of taxation.

Direct taxation	This includes Income tax, National Insurance and corporation tax – direct taxes are charged on earnings.
Indirect taxation	This includes VAT, excise duties (e.g. on petrol and alcohol), car tax, insurance tax and others.

How does it affect business?

Taxes and business

- Direct taxation is placed on earnings and so a change in the level of say, income tax, will alter the level of consumers' disposable income. An increase in taxation will decrease the demand for most products and services although there are exceptions (see page 24 on rising unemployment).

- Indirect taxation such as VAT will have a similar effect; an increase in the rate of VAT will increase the price of many goods and services (food eaten at home and a few other products such as books and children's clothes carry no VAT). This has the effect of decreasing consumption spending.

- Businesses producing goods and services that carry particular taxes, such as fuel and alcohol, may see demand fall if the government increases those taxes.

Financing the new business idea

Businesses need finance for a number of different reasons.

- **Start-up costs** – Starting a new business involves numerous costs. Some of these will be large one-off payments for things like premises and equipment and can be considerable. The business may also need finance to keep paying costs such as wages and raw materials until enough income comes in from its sales.

- **Day to day** – If all goes well, the business will be successful and make a profit. However, this does not mean that the business will have enough cash on a day to day basis to pay its bills. It may well need additional finance to provide sufficient working capital to cope with any cash flow problems.

- **Expansion** – There may come a time when the business will want to expand. This may involve extra finance to pay for it.

Finance is available from a number of sources. Each source has its advantages and disadvantages for the business and each will be the most appropriate in different situations. Businesses must decide between a range of **Internal** and **External** sources of finance.

They mean what they say…	if the finance comes from **inside** the business it is **Internal**.
	if the finance comes from **outside** the business it is **External**.

Internal sources	External sources
Owner's equity	Trade credit
Retained profits	Overdrafts
Sale of assets	Hire purchase/Leasing
	Loans
	Venture capital
	Share capital
	Debenture

Internal sources of finance

- **Owner's equity** – the money that the owner(s) have available to put into the business.

- **Retained profit** – it is all the money that is left after all deductions have been taken away from total sales revenue including tax, interest and any dividends paid to shareholders. It can then be re-invested into the business.

- **Sale of assets** – the business sells assets (things of value e.g. buildings, land, vehicles) in order to raise money. The business will often lease the assets back again.

The great advantage of internal finance is that it will usually cost less than external finance because interest payments will be lower. When owners put in their own finance, they are losing only the interest that the money might have made in a savings account. (This is the opportunity cost of the funds.) Interest rates paid to savers are always lower than the interest rates charged to borrowers. Similarly, retained profits are the savings of the company. They have an opportunity cost but the interest lost will be less than interest that would have to be paid on a loan from the bank.

Selling assets that are not being fully utilised frees up cash. There may be selling costs but there will be no interest to pay. Retained profit is like the owners' personal savings – there is an opportunity cost.

Sources of finance

External sources of finance

- **Trade Credit** – the period of time allowed by a business after supplying another business with goods or services before payment is due, commonly 30 days. In this time the receiving business can use the money internally before finally paying the bill.

- **Overdraft** – a facility from the bank that allows a business to spend more than it has in its account up to an agreed limit. A flexible and useful form of finance that is particularly suited to cash flow problems. Interest is only paid on the amount borrowed and the time it is used.

- **Leasing** – a long term rental agreement that allows businesses to use assets without having to pay for them, thereby freeing up funds for other uses. Often used for vehicles, machinery, photocopiers etc.

- **Hire Purchase** – similar to leasing except that at the end of the agreement the asset becomes the property of the business.

- **Loan** – the use of someone else's money for a period of time. Usually involves regular repayments and the additional payment of interest.

- **Venture Capital** – funding provided by specialist firms or individuals (think Dragon's Den) in return for a proportion of the company's shares. Venture capital investments are seen as relatively high risk because they are unsecured. They also involve a higher rate of interest to compensate for the risk involved.

- **Share capital** – finance raised by selling shares in the company. This can apply both to a private and public limited company.

- **Debenture** – a form of external finance for a business that takes the form of a long term loan often secured on the company's property. It is the business equivalent of a mortgage.

Costs of finance

External sources of finance will have varying costs, just as internal sources do. Loans from family members will cost less than a bank loan, if the lenders are happy with the interest rate they would have got from their savings account with the bank. Share capital is valuable; if in a bad year, the business makes no profit, it does not have to pay a dividend. Of course in a good year, the entrepreneur will have to share the profits with other shareholders. Both risks and returns are being shared by all the shareholders. Trade credit is useful but can cut both ways: the business can delay payment to suppliers but may find that customers want trade credit for themselves. Overdrafts are useful to provide a buffer when there is a temporary shortage of cash with which to pay bills, but they are too expensive to use for major start-up spending.

As a general rule, the cost of finance reflects the risk involved. Big businesses can usually get cheaper loans than small businesses, because they are well-established and unlikely to fail. New businesses may have to pay premium interest rates just because their lack of experience makes them risky. Sometimes banks refuse loans altogether if they feel the risks are too great.

Loans usually involve regular repayments including interest.

Source of finance	Advantages	Disadvantages	Best for...
Owners equity	Does not have to be repaid – no interest	Starting a business is risky – owner may lose all their savings/wealth	Starting a business
Retained profit	Does not have to be repaid – no interest	Can be limited, particularly in the early years – not available for a new business	Expansion of the business
Sale of assets	Does not have to be repaid – no interest – Can be good to dispose of underused assets	Once sold assets are gone, they may be useful in the future – not available for a new business	Raising money quickly
Trade credit	No interest	Limited amounts and only a short term solution – if payment delayed for too long supplier may cut off credit	Good for short term cash flow problems
Overdraft	Flexible – you only pay interest on amount borrowed for as long as overdraft is needed	Interest charges usually higher than loans – not suitable for long term or large amounts	Short term cash flow problems
Leasing	Assets obtained without large expenditure – often with maintenance included – new models regularly updated	More expensive than buying outright in long term – asset never yours – interest paid, regular monthly repayments	Items such as vehicles, photocopiers – medium term finance
Hire purchase	Assets obtained with-out large expenditure – yours to keep at end of rental period	More expensive than buying outright in long term – interest paid, regular monthly repayments	Items such as vehicles, machinery – medium term finance
Loans	Fixed sum available – easy to plan for fixed repayments	Interest paid, regular payments must be made regardless of cash flow – usually need security in case of defaulting on loan	Medium term finance and expansion
Venture capital	Immediate cash injection – if given in exchange for share of business does not need repayment	Venture capitalist may want share of the business in return (loss of control for owner) or charge higher interest rates to compensate for increased risk	Often obtainable by businesses deemed too risky for other sources of finance
Share capital	Immediate cash injection, does not need repayment	Loss of control as more people own a share of the business – need to share profits or make dividends	Long term or large expansions
Debenture	Immediate sum available, repayments spread over a long time, interest rates can be lower	Secured against property – interest paid, regular payments must be made regardless of cash flow	Very long term for large expansions

Business structures

All businesses need a legal structure and there are advantages and disadvantages to each type. Which one a business chooses will depend upon its particular situation and needs. The most common types are **sole trader**, **partnership**, **private limited company** and **public limited company**.

Limited liability

> But first, a word about **liability**…
>
> **Liability** means responsibility for the financial debts of the business.
>
> **Sole traders** and **partnerships** have **unlimited liability** which means that the owners have a legal duty for all debts and can have all of their personal possessions seized to pay the debts.
>
> For **limited companies** their **liability is limited** to the business itself and not the owners/shareholders. The company may lose its assets but the personal wealth of the owners is protected.

Limited liability is a very important factor for most people setting up businesses. Without it, many people would feel unable to go into business on their own because the risks to their families would be too great to contemplate. A hairdresser who starts a business as a sole trader, with £5,000, and eventually goes bankrupt owing £75,000, will personally have to pay back all the debts and may have to sell personal possessions such as a house to do so. If it was a limited company, the hairdresser would only lose their original £5,000 share capital.

Sole traders

- **Sole trader** – an individual who runs his or her own business. They are self employed and usually run small businesses e.g. plumbers, builders, hairdressers. They have full responsibility for the running of the business. Setting up the business is easy and accounts are confidential. Liability is unlimited.

- **Partnerships** – when two or more people start a business together, common examples include solicitors, accountants and dentists. Usually follow the rules laid down in a partnership agreement. Partners are jointly responsible for the running of the business, otherwise the same as a sole trader.

- **Limited companies** – a business has to go through a legal process called incorporation to turn itself into a limited company and become registered with Companies House. It is then owned by its shareholders and run by its directors. Liability is limited to the size of the owner's shareholding. There are two types of limited company.

Private Limited Company – ltd.	Public Limited Company – plc
Company name ends in ltd.	Company name ends in plc
Cannot sell shares to the public	Can sell shares to the public
Shares not listed on stock exchange	Shares listed on stock exchange
Shares cannot be sold without the agreement of other shareholders	Shares can be freely bought and sold
Usually small companies (there are exceptions e.g. Virgin) – no minimum share capital requirements	Usually large companies – need at least £50,000 of share capital
Have to publish accounts and disclose some information	Have to publish and make available full and detailed accounts

Advantages and disadvantages

Financing start-ups

Different business structures have pros and cons that are often closely connected to their financial needs. Business start-ups need to be as uncomplicated as possible because they will be small. If the risks are low, operating as a sole trader or a partnership is the simplest of all. But this will only work if very little finance is needed. As soon as significant start-up costs have to be covered, any reasonable entrepreneur will want **limited liability**. Initially, the entrepreneur will hope to get adequate finance from personal savings and funds contributed by family and friends (either as shares or loans), because these are the cheapest sources of finance. But generally, bank loans will be needed too, for working capital and for investment in production facilities.

PLCs

Becoming a public limited company opens up the possibility of selling shares to the wider public. But it is complex and expensive to launch a plc, and the original owners of the business may not like losing some overall control. Besides, an IPO (initial public offering of the shares) will require expensive advice from banks that specialise in supervising the process. If the general public is not enthusiastic about buying the shares, the IPO may be an expensive flop.

Over time, a growing business will probably consider all the sources of finance. Venture capital may be obtainable when the business is becoming medium sized, but is still deemed rather risky by the banks. But to get it, the business will need a very convincing business plan.

Business structure	Advantages	Disadvantages
Sole trader	Total control, keeps all the profit, simple and easy to set up	No-one to share the work or responsibility, difficult to take holidays or sick leave, high levels of risk (unlimited liability)
Partnership	A partner may bring more start-up capital and extra skills/abilities – a partner can share the workload and responsibility and make it easier to take holidays or sick leave	A partnership still has unlimited liability and each partner is individually liable if the other(s) cannot pay – partners can disagree and fall out – profits are shared
Private limited company	The company has limited liability and so the owner(s) are not personally liable for debts	More complex to set up – limited liability can mean that sources of finance require personal guarantees from the owner(s) so there is still a risk of personal loss – homes may be used as collateral for bank loans
Public limited company	Limited liability and access to share capital	Most complex of all to set up – full accounts must be published – shareholders will want dividends – loss of control for original owner(s)

Estimating sales revenue

All businesses new or otherwise need to know how much profit (or loss) they are making. This means that they need to be able to estimate their sales revenue and costs.

New business start-ups face very great uncertainty. On average, just one in seven new products will be a success. Some businesses will succeed with products that are really not new, but will be competing for a share of an existing market, as with restaurants in a location which has several already. This can work but the newcomer has to be good to compete.

Sales levels are very hard to predict. But realistic estimates are necessary. The quantity sold will depend on the price charged so consideration of pricing strategies is important. Costs are easier to determine, although there is always a risk that they may rise unexpectedly. With a pricing strategy, an estimate of likely sales and the costs involved, it is possible to estimate the likely **profit**. Once that is determined, entrepreneurs can identify all the likely risks and begin to think about what contingency plans might be required.

Pricing strategies

> A **pricing strategy** is the way in which a business decides upon the price of its product or service.

This will depend on a range of factors…

- How much competition will the business have?

- What competitive advantages will the product have? Will it have attractive distinguishing features? Is it in any way differentiated from competing products?

- Is the economy growing?

With a long established product, the decision will be affected by its position in the market. If it is a market leader, it may be possible to charge a relatively high price and rely on brand loyalty to maintain sales. But with a new and unknown business, the price has to be reasonably competitive, in order to establish a reputation.

Businesses may consider a range of strategies:

- **Competitive pricing** – this means looking at the prices that your competitors are charging and making yours similar or slightly less than theirs. This is often done where the competing products are similar in nature.

- **Cost-plus pricing** – the price is decided by calculating how much percentage profit the business wants to make. This is then added on to the total costs of that product e.g. a business wanting to make 20% profit with an average cost of £10 per unit would set the price at £12.

- **Penetration pricing** – a lower price than the competition is set by a new competitor to persuade customers of other products to give their own product a try, in an attempt to penetrate the market and gain market share. Once established, the new entrant will probably raise their price back to a competitive level.

- **Premium pricing** – a higher price is charged than the competition because the product is seen as being more desirable and/or of better quality. This can work for branded or innovative products such as Coca Cola or Apple products but may not be helpful for a new product from an unknown business.

Pricing

- **Price skimming** – skimming the market means charging a very high initial price for the product. This only works for products that are really new and different. Demand will be high and some people will be willing to pay the high price to acquire the unique product. As more competitors enter the market the price will fall. Current examples include 3-D televisions and the latest iPhone. Here again this strategy is more likely to work for a well-established, well-known business.

- **Predatory pricing** – this means setting the price below the cost of production in an attempt to drive rivals out of the market. In the UK it is illegal.

> **Try this**
> Which of the above pricing strategies are most likely to work in the context of a business start-up? Explain your answer.

Sales levels, costs and profit

Profit

Profit is the difference between the value of the total sales revenue of a business and the total costs involved in producing that output. It is **Total Revenue minus Total Costs → TR – TC**.

Of course, if Total Revenue is less than Total Costs, a **loss** will be made.

> Total Revenue (TR) is the value of the sales of a business, sometimes referred to as sales revenue or just turnover.
>
> **Total revenue = Price x Quantity → TR = P x Q**

> Total Costs (TC) are all the costs involved in producing a good or a service. They can be split into two main types, Fixed Costs and Variable Costs (FC and VC)
>
> **Total Costs = Total Fixed Costs (TFC) + Total Variable Costs (TVC) → TC = TFC + TVC**

Fixed costs

Fixed Costs (FC)	These costs **do not change** with output
	Examples include: rent, business rates, loan repayments, manager's salaries.

Variable costs

Variable Costs (VC)	These costs **do change** with output
	Examples include: raw material costs, packaging, energy bills and wage costs where the number of people employed changes with output levels.
	Total Variable Costs will be the cost per unit of output x quantity produced

> **Try this**
> A dairy farmer makes his own ice cream, each tub of ice cream sells for £4.50p. The farmer estimates that the fixed costs each month will be £1,200, the VC of each tub will be £3.00. He hopes that sales for the month of June will be 1000 tubs of ice cream.
>
> How much profit will he make in June? What will happen if it rains a lot and he only sells 600 tubs?

The Break Even Point (BEP)

Profit and break-even

> The **Break Even Point** is the level of output at which the Total Revenue is exactly the same as the Total Costs. At that point, neither a profit nor a loss is being made.
>
> **TR = TC**

When output is **above the break-even point** the business will start to make a profit.

When output is **below the break-even point** the business will start to make a loss.

How to calculate the break-even point

$$\text{Break-even point} \quad = \quad \frac{\textbf{fixed costs}}{\textbf{Contribution (P – VC)}}$$

Figure 9: The break-even level of output

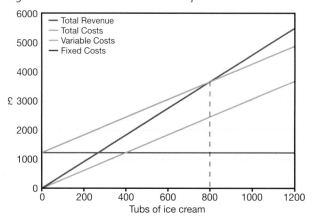

The BEP can be shown by plotting the cost and revenue curves on a graph. The BEP is where TC and TR intersect.

Contribution

Contribution is the difference between the price of a product and its variable costs → **P – VC**

Every time a product is sold, the contribution from its sale can be used to help pay off the fixed costs of the business. Once break-even point is reached, the contribution from the next sale begins to create profit.

> *Try this*
>
> Returning to our dairy farmer who makes his own ice cream, each tub of ice cream sells for £4.50p. The farmer estimates that the fixed costs each month will be £1200, the VC of each tub are £3.00p.
>
> His monthly break-even point will be…
>
> $$\text{BEP} = \frac{\text{FC}}{\text{Contribution (P – VC)}} \quad \rightarrow \quad \frac{£1200}{(£4.50 – £3.00)} \quad \rightarrow \quad \frac{£1200}{£1.50} = 800 \text{ tubs of ice cream}$$
>
> After a very wet June, the farmer decides to reduce the price. His freezers are full and he needs to sell more in order to use the milk he is producing. He decides to reduce the price to £4.
>
> What will happen to the contribution figure?
>
> How will this affect the break-even point?
>
> What will have to happen to make the break-even point achievable?
>
> How promising do you think this business looks?

Contribution gives us another way to calculate profit. The break-even level of output is 800 tubs at a price of £4.50. If sales are 1000 tubs, then the profit = (1000 – 800) x contribution, because for each of the tubs beyond BEP, the contribution is profit.

(1000 – 800) x £1.50p = £300

Margin of safety

The margin of safety is the difference between the actual level of output and the break-even level of output. In our example above it would be 200 tubs of ice cream. Another way to see it is that it shows by how much sales can fall before the business makes a loss. Generally, the greater the margin of safety the better position the business is in.

Is the break-even level of output achievable in the example above? This is a crucial question for anyone thinking of starting a business. Thought must be given to what has to happen to make it *possible* to break even. This will help to clarify both the risks and the precautions that may need to be in place. You might conclude that better advertising strategies are required, or perhaps more freezer capacity.

Break-even analysis

Using break-even analysis

Break-even analysis means looking at the break-even point and deciding if the business venture will be feasible. Different prices and costs can be considered to see how the BEP changes, profit levels can be worked out over a range of outputs. Break-even analysis will be a key element in the business plan if the business is trying to raise finance.

Strengths of break-even analysis	Weaknesses of break-even analysis
Helps to assess the strength of a business idea and whether it is worthwhile or not	The model assumes that costs rise steadily, but they may not; bulk buying can reduce cost per unit
Helps to assess the levels of output that need to be reached to make a profit	The model assumes that all output is sold, in reality this may not happen
Shows the impact of changes in price and/or costs on the BEP and any profit levels	It is only a forecast and estimates of costs and price levels may be wrong or inaccurate
Enables the calculation of profit/loss over different levels of output	Knowing what the BEP is does not mean that you will actually be able to sell that amount
Helps support an application for finance	Markets are dynamic (constantly changing) so that even if your estimates are accurate something else can happen to spoil things e.g. new competition, economic recession etc.

Basic profit and loss

All businesses need to keep some financial records, not just for the taxman but for their own planning and monitoring needs. There is a legal requirement to produce an income statement, but in any case, businesses need to know if they are profitable or not. If profit is declining then that is a signal that something must be done quickly to put things right.

Measuring profit

When a business receives income from the sale of its products (turnover), it has various items it must pay for (the costs) before it can work out how much profit is being made. Just to complicate things, businesses may use different terms to describe the same thing. Remember that turnover, sales revenue and total revenue all mean the same thing. Variable costs and cost of sales both mean the costs that vary with the level of output. And just in case you come across it, there is a third term for this, direct costs. Fixed costs have another name too – overheads. You need to know all these terms because people in business will use different terms when speaking to you.

Profit can be measured in different ways. The two important ones for this Unit are **Gross Profit** and **Operating Profit**. These are not two different ways of describing the same thing – operating profit allows for all costs, whereas gross profit only allows for variable costs.

Operating profit is a key ratio when assessing performance.

Gross profit

> **Gross profit is turnover (or sales revenue or total revenue) minus variable costs (cost of sales)**

Gross profit = Turnover – Variable Costs

Although this gives us a useful guide, it does not take into account fixed costs (overheads). We have to take it a step further. Business need to know how much money is left after *all* costs have been paid (i.e. the profit).

Calculating operating profit and profit margins

Operating profit

> **Operating profit is gross profit minus the fixed costs (overheads)**

Operating profit = Turnover – (Fixed + Variable Costs)

Operating profit is a key indicator of business performance and a figure that shareholders will watch very carefully over time.

Profit margins

> A **profit margin** tells the business just what percentage of its turnover is actually profit. It is the ratio of profit to turnover expressed as a percentage.

A profit margin is an example of a financial ratio (a figure calculated from other figures to give useful information to business managers).

Regardless of whether you are calculating a gross or operating profit margin, the formula is the **same**…

$$\frac{\text{Profit}}{\text{Turnover}} \times 100 = \text{The answer will be a \%}$$

Analysing operating profit

Try this

Marks & Spencer   **Financial year 2009-2010 (£ million)**

Turnover	9,536.6
Operating profit	852

$$\frac{\text{Profit}}{\text{Turnover}} \times 100 \quad \rightarrow \quad \frac{£852}{£9,536.6} \times 100 \quad = \textbf{8.9\% operating profit margin}$$

Should M&S be pleased with this level of operating profit?

Operating profit margins vary from industry to industry and also by size. It is acceptable to run a business on a low profit margin if turnover is high. For example supermarkets typically run on a low profit margin of around 5%. This is good if you are Tesco with a turnover of £56.9 billion but not so good if you are a small village shop with a turnover of £80,000!

Operating profit needs to be higher if the business is risky. Supermarkets can do very well with a low profit margin. They buy in enormous quantities of food and other consumer goods. The value they add to them is simply the process of ensuring that stocks are available in a convenient place and at convenient times to meet the needs of consumers. Most customers' spending will be fairly stable over time and sudden changes are unlikely. A risky business, like oil, will need a higher profit margin to survive. It has to fund expensive exploration, some of which will fail to find much oil. And something may go horribly wrong, as it did for BP in the Gulf of Mexico.

Many business start-ups make a loss at the beginning, and have a rather small profit margin for the first year or two – or maybe more. It is important for them to have sufficient finance to survive the difficult early stages, until margins improve.

➡ The Golden Rule

By itself a profit margin is not very useful. As with any financial ratio/figure, a profit margin is only meaningful if compared with another figure, either figures for the business from earlier years, or figures from other businesses in a similar situation for the same year.

The operating profit margin for Marks and Spencer of 8.9% does not tell us much, but if we know that for the previous year it was 9.6 %, it straightaway tells us that things are not going quite so well for the business.

Changes in profit margins

Managers will use financial information to assess how well the business is doing. An increase over previous figures indicates that they are on the right track; a decrease is cause for concern and a signal for something to be done. Even an increase can be a worry if it is not as big an increase as its competitors have had.

Putting a business idea into practice

Business plan

> A **business plan** is a document that sets out what the business is, what it does and what it wants to achieve and how it is going to do it. It is normally used as part of an attempt to gain financial backing for the business.

In all businesses careful planning helps to reduce risk and uncertainty. Too many businesses get carried away with the excitement of the idea, do not think everything through carefully enough and then discover the problems when it is too late. The process of creating a business plan helps to ensure that every aspect of the business start-up has been carefully considered.

There is no one way to set out a business plan but there are a number of items that should be in it.

● **Executive summary** – this is a brief overview of the whole plan, designed to give potential financial backers a quick idea of what the business is all about and to persuade them to read on.

● **Your business and its products/services** – this part of the plan sets out your vision for your new business and includes who you are, what you do, what you have to offer and the market you want to address. It should include important information about the nature of the product, what will make it special and what its competitive advantage may be.

● **Your markets and competitors** – you need to explain about your market and the customers you are targeting. This section should also look at your competitors and consider how the market may change. It should be based on detailed market research.

● **The marketing plan** – this section should describe the specific activities you intend to use to promote and sell your products and services. It will also include details of the pricing strategy.

● **Organisational details** – provides detail on the human resources involved, covering your own background and skills and those of your managers and staff. It should identify any strengths and plans to deal with any weaknesses.

● **The production plan** – shows how your business plans to produce and deliver your products/services, with details about premises and equipment needed. It will also explain what inputs are needed and about suppliers and other necessary business relationships.

● **Financial forecasts** – probably the most important section. You will need to provide a set of financial projections which show how the business will get started and operate over the first year or so. These should include a **cash flow forecast**, **break-even analysis** and an **income statement**. It will be important to explain the assumptions you have made about prices, costs and sales revenue, in your forecasts. Information about how you might be able to cope if the forecasts prove to be over-optimistic will be especially helpful here.

● **Existing sources of finance** – anyone who is being asked to help finance the business will want to know what **sources of finance** you already have! Banks seldom lend to entrepreneurs who are not prepared to put their own savings into the business.

Reasons for the business plan

Advantages of a business plan	Disadvantages of a business plan
The act of writing a business plan makes you think very carefully about every aspect of your business before you start. You may come across things you had not previously thought of. Even if you do not want to attract financial backers it is a very worthwhile activity.	Just as with cash flow and break-even analysis the business plan is a forecast. It is very difficult to be totally accurate about future revenues and costs. It is even more difficult to be certain about consumer behaviour and the reactions of your competitors.
Can be crucial in convincing potential investors or lenders that your business idea is a sound one.	Just because the plan says it will happen does not mean it will!

Seeking finance

Sources of finance

All businesses need **working capital**, to cover day-to-day costs when there is little sales revenue. Some businesses otherwise require very little finance. Persuasion is a very small radio production company specialized in making local radio adverts for films on release. Now and then it makes radio programmes for the BBC, and it also devises social media advertising campaigns. At the beginning all the work was done from home. During this time the owner made some savings which became his working capital. After six months they moved to a tiny rented office, where the owner and two employees could work, with a computer each. When they needed to make recordings, freelance actors would work on their ideas in a recording studio hired by the hour. For quite a while very little finance was needed. The private limited company status ensured that the owner could not lose his personal possessions, even if the business failed. The bank provided overdraft facilities for emergencies and they drew on this when one of their customers announced that in the future, payment would be made only after sixty days had elapsed. (Extracting payment from a big customer is a common problem for small businesses.)

Businesses that have expensive equipment needs need more finance. Even a small bakery needs an oven and shelving for the products, spaces to prepare the bread and pastries. But large scale manufacturing for mass markets will operate on a completely different scale. The finance needs in manufacturing businesses are huge and they may have to turn to a range of different sources. Generally, the business will need to be a **public limited company** with access to substantial shareholder funds and several different banks.

What help is available?

- The government provides the Business Link website, which has a wealth of information about all aspects of starting a business. Other kinds of public support are at the time of writing (2011) being reviewed and it is not clear what will emerge. Local enterprise partnerships – Leps – are in the process of being set up and it is rumoured that there will be some money available in the regions where job losses in the public sector are likely to be a particular problem. It remains to be seen how this system will work.

- Some banks are very helpful to small businesses but of course they need to be convinced by a very well prepared business plan.

Income statement

An income statement will be included in a well-developed **business plan**. This is just a record of how much profit or loss a business has made over a period of time. In essence it is just a series of subtractions taking us from all the income a business has received over that time, down to the retained profit it gets to keep.

Income statements were introduced in 2005, replacing the old **profit and loss account**. However, some small businesses still produce a P&L account just as before. The two are in fact very similar. The main differences apply to PLCs, with special provisions that are relevant to large businesses. (Importantly, they require the business to provide figures for continuing businesses. This makes it possible to compare like-for-like figures, and encourages accuracy even when the situation is confused by take-overs and the selling off of subsidiary businesses.)

Interpreting income statements

A typical income statement for a small business might look like this:

		£
	Total revenue	275,340
minus	Cost of sales	148,265
equals	Gross profit	127,075
minus	Overheads	73,810
equals	Operating profit	53,265
minus	Financial cost (interest)	8,700
equals	Profit before tax	45,265
minus	Tax	10,863
equals	Profit after tax	34,402

Retained profit

This statement shows managers how well the business is performing and identifies any areas of concern that need looking at. The most important lines are the **operating profit**, which shows profit after all production costs have been paid, and profit after tax, which shows how much profit is available for shareholders or for future investments in the business. If it is going to be kept for future investment it is called **retained profit** and this can be an important source of finance for future growth.

In a business plan for a new business, an income statement will be an estimate of future earnings and costs to give an idea as to the likely future profitability of the business.

Cash flow forecast

Cash flow forecasting

Cash to a business is the equivalent of oil to an engine; without it the business or engine will seize up and grind to a halt. Cash needs to be constantly circulating around the business, which is why it is referred to as a flow.

Cash inflows are the monies gained from sales, finance and any other income the business has. Cash outflows are payments made for all the costs of a business such as materials, labour, rent, capital costs and loan repayments.

A cash flow forecast is an attempt to look at the flows of cash in and out of a business over a period of time. If more money is coming into the business than going out then you have a positive cash flow. If more money is going out of the business than coming in then you have a negative cash flow.

It helps to predict the times when there may be a shortage of cash and therefore a need to arrange a suitable form of finance (normally an overdraft). It takes the form of a spreadsheet showing month by month what is happening to cash entering and leaving the business.

Interpreting cash flow

A sample cash flow forecast – figures in brackets mean a minus figure:

	January £	February £	March £	April £	May £	June £
Cash inflow						
Opening balance	0	1,000	1,500	3,000	(500)	0
Sales revenue	5,000	11,000	13,000	14,000	15,000	16,000
Loans	10,000					
Total cash inflow	15,000	11,000	13,000	14,000	15,000	16,000
Cash outflow						
Stock	8,000	8,000	9,000	11,000	12,000	12,000
Wages	2,000	2,000	2,000	2,000	2,000	2,000
Advertising	1,000			1,000		
Loan repayment	0	500	500	500	500	500
Rent	3,000			3,000		
Total cash outflow	14,000	10,500	11,500	17,500	14,500	14,500
Net cash flow	1,000	500	1,500	(3,500)	500	1,500
Closing balance	1,000	1,500	3,000	(500)	0	1,500

Here a new business starts up with a loan of £10,000, sales are low but with the loan £15,000 comes into the business. Costs need to be paid including the first 3 months rent and some advertising, so £14,000 has left the business meaning that the net cash flow is £1,000 (£15,000 – £14,000). This forms the opening balance for the next month.

Negative cash flow

As sales increase so do some of the costs and all is well until April, when the next quarter's rent falls due and some more advertising is bought. There is a negative cash flow and the balance is a minus figure. Having produced this forecast the business can plan for this, arrange an overdraft and show that after this month the business is once again experiencing a positive cash flow.

> **➡ But...**
>
> Cash flow forecasts are like weather forecasts! They can be inaccurate and the further ahead you try and predict, the greater the error is likely to be. They are predictions; sales may not be as high as expected, costs may change, business rivals may react and affect your planning, the economy might go into a downturn, the government may increase taxes and so on. Nevertheless they are a useful guide and essential to a business plan and any application for finance.

The key factor here is the early warning that the cash flow forecast gives of the need for more finance to cover costs.

A business plan, just like your own revision plan for your exams, needs to be done carefully and realistically. It then has to be followed without any short cuts! Good luck!

Glossary of key terms in Unit 1

Added value – the difference between the price of a good or service and the cost of its material inputs.

Assets – anything that is useful or valuable to a business. Assets can be physical such as buildings, machines etc. or they can be intangible such as a brand name or the skills of the workforce.

Autocratic management – a style of management where decisions are made by the owner or manager of the business, with little or no consultation with others. Disagreement or discussion is not encouraged. Employees are expected to follow orders without question.

Bank loan – a fixed sum of money borrowed from a bank and repaid with regular monthly repayments plus interest over a fixed period.

Brand – the name or symbol that is closely associated with a product or service. Brands add value, increase consumer loyalty and enable a higher price to be charged.

Break-even point – the level of output where neither a profit nor a loss is being made. The point at which Total Revenue equals Total Costs.

Break-even point calculation – the formula is $\dfrac{\text{Fixed Costs}}{\text{Contribution (P} - \text{VC)}}$

Business plan – a formal document that sets out the details of the business. It acts as a planning aid for the business itself and as a means of attracting potential investors or providers of finance. It will also usually include a marketing plan and financial plans including an income statement and a cash flow forecast.

Cash flow – the movement of cash into (cash inflow) and out of (cash outflow) a business. The cash inflow must be sufficient to cover the cash outflow in any given month so careful management is needed to avoid running out of cash at crucial times.

Cash flow forecast – a spreadsheet that projects expected flows of cash income and cash expenditure month by month. It will help to identify times when cash may be short and allow the business to make plans to deal with it.

Collateral – anything of value that can be seized by a lender if a loan is not repaid. Collateral is often property. (Sometimes called security.)

Competitive advantage – any feature of a business that enables it to compete effectively. It may be based on price, quality, service, reputation or innovation.

Competitive pricing – a pricing strategy that consists of matching your competitor's prices or slightly undercutting them.

Complementary goods – goods that tend to be bought together e.g. cars and petrol, DVDs and DVD players.

Consumer Price Index (**CPI**) – one measure of the rate of inflation based on price changes of a wide range of goods and services thought to be typical of the 'average consumer'.

Contribution – price minus variable cost (P – VC). This can be used to calculate the break-even point.

Cost of sales – another way of describing variable costs or direct costs, they are subtracted from turnover to give gross profit.

Cost-plus pricing – a pricing strategy that adds a given percentage increase onto total costs to arrive at a selling price.

Creditor – a person or company that the business owes money to, usually in exchange for materials or services. Failure to pay creditors can result in legal action being taken by the creditor.

Debenture – a form of external finance for a business, it is a long term loan often secured on the company's property.

Demand – the amount of a good or service that consumers are willing and able to buy, at a given price and at a given time.

Demand curve – a graphical representation of the relationship between price and quantity demanded.

Democratic management – a style of management where decisions are made by a manager after consulting with colleagues and taking into account differing points of view.

Disposable income – the amount of income a person has left to actually spend on goods and services. It measures consumers' spending power after tax and other outgoings have been accounted for.

Entrepreneur – a person who takes the risk of setting up, organizing and operating a business venture. It usually carries the connotation of being creative, self-motivated, and visionary.

Equilibrium price – the price at which quantity demanded is the same as quantity supplied, sometimes called the market clearing price.

Exchange rate – the price of one currency expressed in terms of another, e.g. the exchange rate of the pound in terms of the dollar might be $1.70.

Exports – goods and services sold by one country to other countries.

Fixed costs – those costs or expenses incurred by a business that do not change with the level of output. Examples include rent, interest payments, managers' salaries and business rates.

Government spending – the money spent in the economy over a period of time on a range of publicly provided goods and services such as education, healthcare and social security. Spending for the year 2011-12 was forecast to be £740 billion. It is mostly mostly financed by taxation.

Gross Domestic Product (GDP) – used as a measure of the economic wealth of a country. The total value of all goods and services produced within the borders of a country within a time period, usually a year.

Gross profit – what is left after the cost of sales has been subtracted from turnover. Overheads (fixed costs), interest and tax have not yet been taken into account.

Gross profit margin – a measure of profitability. Gross profit is shown as a percentage of turnover:

$$\frac{\text{Gross Profit}}{\text{Turnover}} \times 100$$

Imports – goods and services bought by one country from other countries.

Inflation – a sustained rise in the general price level or a fall in the value of money. Expressed as a percentage figure it was 3.2% in late 2010.

Interest rate – a payment in percentage terms for the use of a sum of borrowed money. It can be seen as the price of money.

Japanese way – a general description of the practices and management styles developed by the Japanese that led to greater efficiency and better quality in production. Now adopted by most manufacturers, they are covered in greater detail in Unit 2b.

Laissez faire leadership – a management style that is the opposite of autocratic. A laissez faire manager is usually content to trust his employees and let them make decisions without having to consult.

Leasing – a long term rental agreement that allows businesses to use assets without having to pay for them outright, thereby freeing up funds for other uses. Often used for vehicles, machinery, photocopiers etc.

Limited liability – in the event of financial problems and the closure of a business the responsibility for any outstanding debts is limited to the original investment.

Loan – the use of someone else's money for a period of time. Usually involves regular repayments and the additional payment of interest.

Ltd – signifies a Private Limited Company. This is a form of company organisation with limited liability but whose shares are not available to the public and are not quoted on the stock exchange.

Margin of safety – the difference between the actual level of output and the break-even level of output.

Market – any medium in which buyers and sellers interact and agree to trade at a price.

Market growth – an expansion of the market usually measured in increases in sales.

Market mapping – using a grid showing two features of a market, such as price and consumer age. Individual brands or businesses are added to the grid to show potential niches or gaps in the market. It also helps to show how products are positioned in relation to each other.

Market niche – a small part of an overall market which has certain special characteristics. Usually a specialist product, it may face reduced competition and be able to charge a premium price.

Market orientation – where the needs of the customer are the overriding priority in the production and marketing of products and services.

Market positioning – how individual products or brands are seen in relation to their competitors by the consumers. Businesses may well attempt to re-position their products in an attempt to boost sales.

Market segmentation – the splitting up of the market into groups of consumers with similar characteristics. Common groupings include age, gender, income, interests, location etc. This enables products and services to be designed specifically for and targeted at a particular segment.

Marketing plan – the setting out of a range of strategies that will be used to promote and sell the product or service. This may well include details on price, promotion and distribution.

Mass market – a large market which includes the majority of the relevant population.

Operating profit – the profit made on a business' ordinary trading activities. It is calculated by subtracting all overheads (fixed costs) from gross profit.

Operating profit margin – operating profit shown as a percentage of turnover:
$$\frac{\text{Operating Profit}}{\text{Turnover}} \times 100$$

Opportunity cost – the cost of the next best alternative that has been sacrificed. The opportunity cost of a business buying a new delivery van may be the new computer system that they have had to forego.

Ordinary share capital – the money raised by the selling of ordinary shares in plc businesses. These are stakes in the business and the shareholders will receive a dividend (if the business is profitable!).

Overdraft – a facility that allows a business (or an individual) to borrow up to an agreed limit. A flexible and useful form of finance, it is particularly suited to dealing with cash flow problems. Interest is only paid on the amount borrowed and for the time it is used.

Partnership – when two or more people start a business together and have unlimited liability. Partners are jointly responsible for the running of the business.

Paternalistic – a leadership style that is based on a 'fatherly' approach. It is closely linked to an autocratic approach. Decisions will usually be discussed but ultimately, the final decision will come from the top. However it will take the needs of the workforce into account.

Penetration pricing – a lower price than the competition is set by a new competitor to try and gain market share.

Premium price – a higher price than the competition because the product is seen as being more desirable and/or of better quality.

Plc – stands for Public Limited Company. This is a form of company organisation with limited liability but whose shares are available to the public and are quoted on the stock exchange.

Price skimming – skimming the market means charging a very high initial price for a new product, taking advantage of there being little competition at the beginning.

Pricing strategy – the decision made by a business as to what its price will be. Many factors influence this decision such as the costs of production, the level of competition, the desirability of the product, the need to break into a market and external economic factors.

Primary research – the gathering of original information about the market from first hand sources. Sometimes called Field Research.

Private sector – that part of the economy which is both run for private profit and is not controlled by the state. It is owned by individuals.

Product trial – launching a product or service in a small area in order to assess likely demand levels in the market as a whole. This may involve heavy promotion, particularly where there are already many existing similar brands.

Production plan – the details of how a product or a service is to be developed and produced for consumption.

Profit – the difference between total sales revenue and total costs.

Profit and loss account – a financial document that shows the amount of profit (or loss) that a firm has made over a period of time. It has now been largely replaced by the income statement.

Public sector – industries or services provided or funded by the government and not owned by private individuals.

Qualitative research – a market research method that involves finding out about the motivation of consumers e.g. *why* consumers might prefer a blue car to a red car.

Quantitative research – a market research method that involves numerical measurement e.g. *how many* consumers might prefer a blue car to a red car.

Retained profit – an important source of finance to businesses. It is all the money that is left after all deductions have been taken away from total sales revenue, including any dividends paid to shareholders. It can then be re-invested in the business.

Revenue – the income of a business raised by selling its goods or services.

Secondary research – the use of information that already exists about the market from other sources. Sometimes called Desk Research.

Sole trader – the simplest form of business organisation that is owned and operated by an individual. The owner has unlimited liability.

Stakeholder – any individual or group with an interest in the actions of a business. Stakeholders include: employees, owners & shareholders, customers, suppliers and the local community.

Substitute – a good or a service that can be used in place of another, e.g. different brands of washing powder or makes of television.

Supply – the amount of a good or service that producers are willing and able to provide, at a given price and at a given time.

Supply curve – a graphical representation of the relationship between price and quantity supplied.

Taxation – payments made to the Government by a wide range of people and businesses. It provides the revenue needed to finance Government spending. The level of taxation can be varied to influence the economy. Commonly used taxes include: income tax, VAT, corporation tax and excise duty.

Theory X – a managerial approach described by McGregor. Theory X managers believe that workers are inherently lazy and dislike work, they need to be directed and coerced and they will avoid responsibility. It does not describe the workers themselves but the manager's attitude towards them.

Theory Y – a managerial approach described by McGregor. Theory Y managers believe that workers are inherently trustworthy and respond to responsibility, in fact, the opposite viewpoint to Theory X. It does not describe the workers themselves but the manager's attitude towards them.

Trade credit – the period of time allowed by a business before payment is due, after supplying a customer. Commonly 30 days. It helps the customer's cash flow at the expense of the business'.

Trade-off – a situation where having more of one thing leads to less of another. It is linked to the concept of opportunity cost. For example, a business may want to pay higher wages but this may mean that profits and dividend payments to shareholders will be lower.

Turnover – the total income generated by a business' sales of its goods and services over a period of time.

Unemployment – the problem of people (or resources) that are not working. This means that the economy is not producing as much as it could. The level of unemployment is measured as a percentage of the workforce. There are several different ways of measuring this and care must be taken when making comparisons.

Unique Selling Point (**USP**) – anything about a product or service that distinguishes it from its competitors.

Unlimited liability – the owner(s) of a business is (are) responsible for all the debts of a business should it fail. This applies to sole traders and partnerships.

Variable costs – costs of production that vary with the level of output e.g. raw materials and distribution costs.

Venture capital – A form of business finance, unsecured funding provided by specialist firms in return for a proportion of the company's shares. Venture capital investments are seen as relatively high risk because they are unsecured. They also involve a higher rate of interest to compensate for the possible risk.

Working capital – the finance needed to cover business costs when sales revenue is slow to come in.

The nature of markets

> A **market** is any medium in which buyers and sellers interact and agree to trade at a price.

Dynamic markets

Markets can be real or virtual, small or global. The key characteristic is that buyers and sellers following their own interests create market forces that determine both the price and quantity sold of a good or service.

- **Buyers** – are all those people or organisations that want to purchase something; they create the **demand** for goods and services.

- **Sellers** – are all those people or organisations that want to sell something; they create the **supply** of goods and services.

> Markets are said to be **dynamic**. This means that they are constantly changing. Countless decisions made at the individual level by both buyers and sellers alter the nature and behaviour of the market. Sellers respond to the changing needs of buyers by improving existing products and services or introducing new ones. Sellers respond to other seller's changes in order to remain competitive.

Any business has to adapt to the changing nature of its market. If it does not, it is likely to get left behind and cease to be competitive. Ultimately falling sales will cause it to exit the market. Markets are dynamic because they are shaped by market forces.

Some markets are more dynamic than others. Most high-tech products have rapidly changing markets. Here the dynamism has its origins in the changes in technology on the supply side of the market. Some businesses create new products, or new variations of an older product (think of smart phones). Other businesses make well-known products in new ways, with **new technologies** that help them to cuts costs of production. (Think of salmon – fish farming cut costs and created a mass market.)

New substitutes

Dynamism can start on the demand side of the market too. A change in fashions will lead to rising demand for some products and falling demand for others. Advertising may change tastes and fashions, or they may change all on their own. Rising incomes can increase demand, especially for luxuries. Demand for some products falls because a more desirable substitute has been found.

Some markets are relatively slow moving, for example the snack confectionery market is dominated by brands. Some are very old – Kit-Kat and Mars bars have survived for 75 years, more or less unchanged.

Markets can be real or virtual, small or global.

Resources

The allocation of resources

In any economic system decisions have to be made as to how to use the resources available. This is known as the allocation of resources.

> Resources are...
> - **Land** – raw materials and land itself
> - **Labour** – the human input
> - **Capital** – anything that is used to produce something else such as tools, equipment and buildings
> - **Enterprise** – the human spark that combines the above and creates a product

There are countless ways in which these resources can be combined to produce countless outcomes in terms of different products and services.

> **So – we have to answer the three basic questions...**
> - What do we produce?
> - How do we produce it?
> - For whom do we produce it?

Market forces

Some forms of government, such as historically, those in the old communist countries of Eastern Europe and today in North Korea and Cuba, did this by central planning i.e. the government decided what and how much would be produced. In a **free market economy** it is the **market forces** of demand and supply that determine the allocation of resources.

> A **free market economy** is one where there is no interference from outside agencies, such as the government. The market forces of demand and supply are allowed to operate freely.

In reality a completely free market economy does not exist. Most countries have a mixed economy, with a varying degree of government intervention and control. Nevertheless market forces remain very powerful in most markets. All businesses and many charities feel their power constantly.

The profit signalling mechanism

Profit signalling

In a free market, resources are allocated by the profit signalling mechanism. Profit is like a beacon that attracts resources towards itself. Entrepreneurs are motivated by profit and are likely to search out markets where profit can be made. The theory works like this...

> Buyers decide what it is they wish to buy
> ↓
> This creates the demand for the product or service
> ↓
> Producers see the chance to make a profit by producing the product or service
> ↓
> Resources are allocated to produce the product or service
> ↓
> This creates supply of the product or service
> ↓
> The existence of profit encourages more businesses to join the industry

Consumer sovereignty

It also works in reverse as well. The absence of profit (loss), means that some resources will stop producing the things people want less and seek out profit elsewhere. Profit (or the lack of it) acts as an incentive to respond to changing demand. In this way resources are constantly being used to provide what consumers most want in the most efficient manner. This is **consumer sovereignty** – the power of the consumer to determine what is produced. It is important because resources are scarce, and it works to give society as a whole the best standard of living possible with the resources available.

It all sounds very neat and plausible but like many economic models it does not always work in real life. It assumes rather optimistically that…

● Buyers and sellers know what is happening in the market.

● Buyers make informed and rational decisions.

● Resources are easily transferred from non-profitable areas to profitable ones.

● Markets are competitive.

● If there is a demand for something the market will provide it.

Competition

In reality there are all sorts of things that interfere with the profit-signalling mechanism. The most problematic of the assumptions above is that **markets are competitive**. People in business think a lot about competition and most of their thoughts focus on how to avoid it. Creating a distinctive product hardly hinders competition – in fact, it often provides consumers with more choices. But when a big business buys a competitor business and rationalises production, its sheer size in the marketplace may give it a lot of influence. It may end in being able to raise prices, or just get careless about keeping costs down to a minimum. Higher prices eat into real incomes. The market will become less competitive and consumer sovereignty may be threatened. Only through competition can prices be kept down to the lowest possible level. We shall return to this!

Changes in demand and supply

> ### ➡ At this stage…
>
> … and before you go any further you should go back to Unit 1 and check your understanding of basic demand and supply theory in section 1.3.2. The rest of this section carries on from there.

Supply and demand

In this Unit you must be able to show and explain what happens to equilibrium price and quantity when there is a change in the conditions of demand or supply.

● A change in the conditions of demand will shift the demand curve to the right or left.

● A change in the conditions of supply will shift the supply curve to the left or right.

Either of these will create a new equilibrium price and quantity.

In the exam…

● You may be asked to show the effect of certain events upon the market for a good or service.

● You will need to decide if these events will shift the demand curve, the supply curve or both.

● You will need to show these changes on a D&S diagram, showing any changes to equilibrium price and quantity.

● You will need to explain in writing your reasoning.

Supply and demand

Question: Draw a diagram showing the market for beef following the BSE crisis

Figure 10: Tracking changes in the market

Step 1: Draw a basic D&S diagram

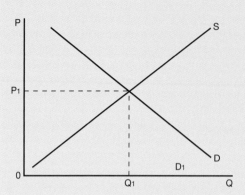

Step 2: Decide which curve(s) is(are) affected

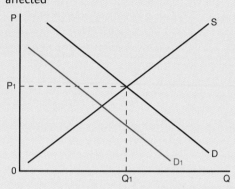

Step 3: Show new equilibrium price and quantity

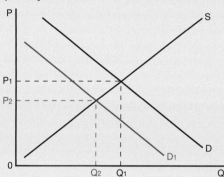

Step 4: Provide a written explanation

Consumers are worried about the health risks in eating beef and may switch to other meats such as pork or lamb (substitutes). There has been a change in tastes and less is now demanded by consumers at each and every price. The demand curve shifts to the left creating a new equilibrium. Price falls from P_1 to P_2 and quantity demanded falls from Q_1 to Q_2.

Try this

Use diagrams and explain what is happening in:

1. The market for bread following an increase in the price of flour.

2. The market for Daz washing powder following an increase in the price of Ariel washing powder.

3. The market for foreign holidays following an increase in income tax.

4. The market for apples following a fine autumn and a bumper harvest.

(Answers on page 110)

Elasticity

Price elasticity

Elasticity can be tricky to understand at first but it is an important concept and explains much economic and business behaviour. You need to understand two types of elasticity – **Price Elasticity of Demand** and **Income Elasticity of Demand**.

Elasticity is all about how much one variable changes in response to a change in another related variable.

Price Elasticity of Demand (PED)

Calculating price elasticity of demand

We know from Unit 1 that a change in price will bring about a change in quantity demanded. What we do not know at the moment is by **how much** the quantity demanded will change. This is what PED is all about.

To compare changes we need to look at proportionate or percentage changes in order to make the comparison meaningful. We can then use a formula to work out PED:

$$PED = \frac{\% \text{ change in quantity demanded}}{\% \text{ change in price}}$$

Price elasticity of demand measures the responsiveness of quantity demanded to a change in price.

Interpreting price elasticity

This will give a numerical answer which tells us the degree of elasticity and we then refer to a good or a service as being price elastic or price inelastic…

Name	What happens	What it means	Numerical value
Price elastic	A price change causes a proportionately **bigger** change in quantity demanded	% change in Q is **greater** than the % change in P	Beyond -1
Unitary price elasticity	A price change causes the **same** proportional change in quantity demanded	% change in Q is the **same** as the % change in P	-1
Price inelastic	A price change causes a proportionately **smaller** change in quantity demanded	% change in Q is **smaller** than the % change in P	Between 0 and -1

➡ But why is the answer negative?

Remember that P and Q move in opposite directions.

If P ↑ then Q must go ↓ and if P ↓ then Q must go ↑. Therefore one variable is always a minus, which means that the answer will also be a minus.

Try this

If a chain of shoe shops reduces the price of a pair of shoes from £50 to £40 and sales per week increase from 100 pairs to 110 it is difficult to measure what has happened. But if we turn these changes into percentages we see that price has dropped by 20% and quantity has increased by 10%…

$$PED = \frac{\% \text{ change in quantity demanded}}{\% \text{ change in price}} \rightarrow \frac{-10\%}{20\%} = -0.5\%$$

So PED is price inelastic

Now do it yourself. The supermarket has bought too much Wensleydale cheese and even with yet another Wallace and Gromit advertising campaign, they have only shifted 50 packets a day at £2.50 each. The next day they cut the price to £2.00 and sell 75 packets. Now they know something about its PED.

What is the PED for this particular cheese?

Was it a good idea to cut the price? Explain your answer.

Why might the PED for cheese be different from the PED for a pair of shoes?

Why is PED important to businesses?

The impact of price elasticity of demand

- **Marketing** – it is extremely important for a business to know what may happen to its demand if it changes the price of its products or services. A business may have to change price for all sorts of reasons: changes in costs, actions of competitors and so on. It needs to know for planning purposes what may happen.

- **Branding** – businesses try to make the demand for their products more price inelastic. They do this by advertising and branding. They try to persuade their customers that there is no acceptable substitute. If they are successful they can increase the price without losing too many sales.

- **Total revenue** – changing price can dramatically affect total revenue, depending upon whether the demand is price elastic or price inelastic. A business needs to know what might happen.

How might price elasticity affect business decisions? Using PED data to predict what might happen to total revenue at different price levels will help with pricing decisions. Sometimes it will be possible to estimate PED using market research data. Otherwise, people in business have to work on a hunch. People with plenty of experience in the markets where they sell can be very good at deciding on a price without actually knowing the formula for PED. But they can also get a nasty surprise if their hunch turns out to be wrong.

Business can use branding to make the demand for their products more price inelastic.

Calculating total revenue

Example

(But first a reminder about how to calculate total revenue from Unit 1. → TR = P x Q)

A business has a PED of -2

It is contemplating putting its price up from £10 to £11

Sales are currently 500 units per week

Price goes up by £1 which is 10%

Using our PED of −2 and the formula, we can work out that the change in Q will be -20%. (Another way to look at it is that -2 means the change in Q will be twice that of P.) So the actual fall in Q will be 100 units, to a new level of 400.

The TR **before** the price change is   £10 x 500 = £5,000

The TR **after** the price change is   £11 x 400 = £4,400

- **With a price elastic good, a price rise reduces TR by £600, because the percentage of people who decide not to buy at the new price is higher than the percentage change in price.**

Let's use the same example only this time the PED is -0.5

A 10% P rise will change sales by -5%, so the actual fall in Q will be 25 units to a new level of 475

The TR **before** the price change is   £10 x 500 = £5,000

The TR **after** the price change is   £11 x 475 = £5,225

- **With a price inelastic good a price rise increases TR by £225.**

Elasticity, demand curves and total revenue

The impact of PED on total revenue

Figure 11: Elastic demand curve

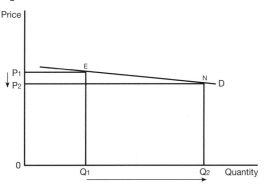

Figure 12: Inelastic demand curve

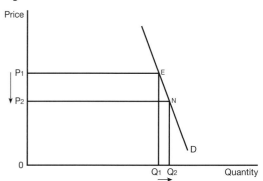

Figure 11 shows an elastic demand curve, i.e. one with a very gentle slope. A cut in price will have a dramatic effect on the quantity sold, just what you would expect if demand is very elastic.

Figure 12 shows an inelastic demand curve (with a very steep gradient). This means that a price cut actually reduces total revenue.

A business that can cut costs and reduce prices in a competitive market is going to do well (as in Figure 11). Demand is elastic. Total revenue will rise dramatically. The business can enlarge its market by attracting customers who previously bought substitutes. (Clearly in the reverse case, if it is not making a profit and tries to raise prices, it will make matters worse.)

A business with a very popular brand and great customer loyalty will be able to raise prices and increase total revenue. Demand is inelastic (as in Figure 12). If it knows that this is how its market is, such a business will certainly not cut prices! With few substitutes, it is effectively safe from competition and has a good deal of control over its price and quantity sold.

In general, increasing price (if possible) is a good thing with price inelastic goods and services, but not if they are price elastic. The seller can charge a higher price without losing sales to a significant extent.

The opposite holds true… in general, decreasing price (if possible) is a bad thing with price inelastic goods and services, but not if they are price elastic.

PED and total revenue

If demand is price elastic	If demand is price inelastic
Increasing price would reduce TR (P ↑ TR ↓)	Increasing price would increase TR (P ↑ TR ↑)
Reducing price would increase TR (P ↓ TR ↑)	Reducing price would decrease TR (P ↓ TR ↓)

The government understands PED very well; that's why it puts indirect taxes on price inelastic goods such as alcohol, cigarettes and petrol and not price elastic ones!

For individual businesses, high price elasticity goes together with being in a highly **competitive market**. Where there are many competing businesses, there will be plenty of good substitutes around. A price increase will be very likely to drive customers away. An obvious answer would be to cut costs and increase efficiency. This would be one way to maintain competitive advantage.

From the consumers' point of view, **competitive markets** and **elastic demand** force businesses to keep costs and prices down to the minimum possible and this is good for their standard of living. But you can see why someone in business may hope that at least some segments of their market will have relatively inelastic demand. To achieve this, businesses will look for any product feature that will stand out and give customers the feeling of getting value for money. *They will try to select a market position for their products where demand is as price-inelastic as possible.*

Factors that affect the degree of price elasticity

Reasons for elastic demand

- **Number and closeness of substitutes** – The more substitutes a product or service has, the more price elastic it will be. The closeness of the substitute is important as well e.g. Nescafé and Maxwell House are quite close substitutes for instant coffees, but tea and coffee, which are both hot drinks, are not close substitutes for many people.

- **Luxury or necessity** – Luxuries tend to be more price elastic and necessities tend to be more price inelastic. (Unless the luxury in question is a status symbol, in which case cutting the price may make it say less about your status.)

- **Proportion of income spent on good** – If a box of matches increases in price by 10% most people will either not notice or not be concerned; sales will hardly change. On the other hand if a new car goes up in price by 10% sales are likely to drop significantly.

- **Time scale** – In the short term many products and services will be more price inelastic than in

The availability of substitutes is a key factor.

the long term. Significant increases in the price of fuel leave consumers with little choice but to keep buying. Over time this will lead to more economical vehicles and the development of alternative energy sources.

> **Try this**
>
> About 20 years ago, when phone calls cost more than they do now and very few people had internet connections, the Post Office was losing money. It was sure that the demand for postage stamps was price inelastic. It decided to increase postage costs by 10% and fully expected to get some extra sales revenue. It was wrong. It turned out that PED was about -1.2%. People economised on sending things by post and revenue fell.
>
> Why might the Post Office have thought that demand was price inelastic?
>
> If the Post Office tries a 10% increase in stamp prices now, will it help to stem the losses?
>
> Do you think that PED has changed? Explain your answer.
>
> What options might be open to the Post Office?

Income Elasticity of Demand (YED)

We know from Unit 1 that a change in income will also bring about a change in quantity demanded. Again, what we do not know at the moment is by **how much** quantity demanded will change. This is what YED is all about.

Calculating income elasticity of demand

The formula used is similar to PED:

> $$YED = \frac{\% \text{ change in quantity demanded}}{\% \text{ change in income}}$$
>
> **Income elasticity of demand** measures the responsiveness of quantity demanded to a change in income.

This will give a numerical answer which tells us the degree of elasticity and we then refer to a good or a service as being income elastic or income inelastic...

Interpreting income elasticity of demand

Name	What happens	What it means	Numerical value
Income elastic	An income change causes a proportionately **bigger** change in quantity demanded	% change in Q is greater than the % change in Y	Greater than 1
Unitary income elasticity	An income change causes the **same** proportional change in quantity demanded	% change in Q is the **same** as the % change in Y	1
Income inelastic	An income change causes a proportionately **smaller** change in quantity demanded	% change in Q is **smaller** than the % change in Y	Between 0 and 1

Normal and inferior goods

➡ **Unfortunately YED is a little more complicated than PED**

For most products and services as incomes rise, quantity demanded also rises and vice versa. These are called **normal goods**. They have a **positive** + YED value.

There are some products and services that do not behave like this – as incomes rise, quantity demanded falls and vice versa. These are called **inferior goods**. They have a **negative** – YED value.

Type of good	Incomes rise ↑	Incomes fall ↓
Normal	Quantity demanded ↑	Quantity demanded ↓
Inferior	Quantity demanded ↓	Quantity demanded ↑

Positive and negative YED

An inferior good is not necessarily of poor quality but is seen as a substitute for more expensive goods. Public transport is seen as an inferior good because if people's incomes fall they are more likely to sell their cars and switch to the bus. If their incomes then rise again, they are likely to buy cars and stop using the bus. Takeaway pizzas are sometimes seen as an inferior good compared to meals eaten out in restaurants.

Businesses selling inferior products and services tend to do well during a recession when incomes tend to fall and consumer confidence is low. Halfords have seen an increase in sales during the recent recession as more motorists do their own maintenance or buy a bike to commute and save money.

By contrast businesses selling luxury income elastic goods tend to do less well when there is an economic downturn. A rise in incomes as an economy recovers and grows tends to have the opposite effect.

Factors that affect the degree of income elasticity
Whether the product or service is a luxury or a necessity.

● Luxuries are income elastic and have high positive values e.g. exotic holidays, designer goods.

● Necessities are income inelastic and have a low positive value e.g. baked beans, petrol.

Why is YED important?

Implications of income elasticity

● Incomes tend to change relatively slowly and individual incomes changing will have little effect on YED. It is when incomes change en masse that it begins to affect a business.

● Businesses may need to react to changes in incomes and plan accordingly. The usual cause of this is a change in the economy e.g. the recession of 2008.

● This meant problems for many sellers of luxury goods and they had to find ways of coping with falling sales. By contrast sellers of inferior goods will have seen rising sales and had to adjust their production accordingly.

Try this

You live on a dairy farm. Milk prices are low and making a profit selling milk is difficult. You have already installed all the labour saving equipment you can. You plan to branch out and start making cheeses. You have a new recipe and know how to make it. You reckon it will command a good price in the local farm shops and can be sent to the specialist cheese shops in London and other big cities. You just have to come up with a pricing strategy.

You are going to advise your parents on this because you know more about these things than they do. What sort of pricing strategy might be appropriate for this business?

Have you any idea what the PED might be for this new cheese? If not, how would you find it out?

How are you going to explain why knowing this might be important?

What will the YED be for a product like this? Does it matter?

Go back to your first answer, on the pricing strategy. Do you want to change anything? Explain why you think it is the right answer (when you think you have got it right).

Marketing in dynamic markets

Responding to changing markets

Markets change all the time. They are dynamic, responding to shifts in demand and supply. Businesses cannot afford to stand still; they must take notice of what is happening.

Successful businesses must have a range of tactics and strategies to deal with the changes in the market. Their marketing plans can be…

- Offensive, in that they try and increase sales or develop new markets.

- Defensive, in that they react to competition and try to maintain their market share.

- A mixture of both.

The objectives of the business will vary. Of course it will want to make a profit. But which is more important, short or long-term gains? If the focus is on the short term, charging a high price may look like a good idea. From a long-term perspective, the business might look to expand, creating a mass market or increasing its market share by keeping prices as low as possible. Becoming more powerful in the market may seem more attractive than making short-term profits. The business may look to add more value or develop a competitive advantage in other ways. **Marketing** will be an important part of this. It can lead to an increase in market share, whether or not the market is dynamic in other ways. This would be an offensive strategy.

Some of the changes that businesses typically face will be external. A competitor may bring a new product to the market which has many attractive features. To compete, the business will have to rethink its own product strategy. (This will be defensive marketing.) Or costs may rise, threatening all the businesses in this particular market. The winner may be the business that can compete on price, absorbing the cost increases successfully by looking for ways of improving efficiency.

> **Marketing** is the action or process of promoting and selling products or services, including market research and advertising. It is how the business connects to its customers.

In order to adapt effectively, businesses need to know what is going on in the market and its wider environment and then constantly adapt and update their marketing mix. How they respond will depend a good deal on the type of business and its size and position in the market. This section will look at the ways in which different businesses might adapt to market change. But to do this you need a good grasp of the basic techniques of marketing.

> ➡ **Many of the ideas that were covered in Unit 1 are relevant here**
>
> You should check your understanding of…
>
> - Market research
> - Market mapping and positioning
> - Market orientation
> - Market segmentation
> - Product orientation
> - Pricing strategies

The marketing mix

**Marketing
strateties**

The marketing mix is a term used to describe those tactics and strategies that a business uses to promote and sell its products or services. It can also be described as the **4 P's**...

- **Price**

- **Product**

- **Promotion**

- **Place**

Price

The ability to set price can be a valuable source of **competitive advantage**. For many consumers price is an important factor when deciding which product to choose. It may be that being the cheapest is important. Alternatively, a high price may denote exclusivity and desirability. The **pricing strategy** is almost always an important aspect of marketing.

Product

Adding value

For some consumers the product itself will be the most important factor when deciding which product to choose. High tech products sell themselves on their features. The shelf life of a Smartphone or digital camera is relatively short, as new models and/or versions regularly appear to tempt the consumer. Price becomes less important. Design, reliability and personal tastes may be important aspects of the choice. Features that add value to the product could enhance its competitiveness in a dynamic market. Businesses may consider their product positioning very carefully and deliberately create a differentiated product that is distinctive enough to attract a larger share of the market.

Promotion

This refers to any tactic used to bring a product or service to a consumer's attention and then persuade them to buy it. There is a whole range of promotional techniques out there including price reductions, special offers, advertising in all its forms, sponsorship and direct selling.

Place

This is all about getting the product or service to the consumer at the right time and place. It is about making the product easily accessible and available for the consumer to buy. The internet has radically altered many of the traditional ways in which this can be done. But many traditional retail outlets still work well alongside the newer systems.

The mix

**Market
changes**

It is called the marketing **mix** because the ingredients will be used together in different combinations depending upon the needs and characteristics of a particular market.

The mix will be adapted in response to changes in the market such as...

- Changes in consumer behaviour.

- Actions of competitors.

- Emerging technologies.

- Problems with costs.

- External economic influences.

Selecting the right marketing mix

Price

More important	Less important
● When launching a new product or entering a new market	● If the product has little competition
● For products with a lot of competition	● If there is a strong brand
	● When producers accept the going market price

Product

More important	Less important
● For high tech products such as phones	● Standardised or mass market products where price is critical
● When quality or reliability are important to consumers	
● To differentiate product from the competition	

Promotion

More important	Less important
● When the product is new	● If there are few competitors
● When sales are declining	● Consumers are already aware of the product
● When competition is high	

Place

More important	Less important
● Launching new products	● Internet has made physical place less important.
● Consumers need to see and be aware of product.	

Non-price competition

The marketing mix highlights the whole range of strategies for competing, not just price. Many businesses spend time on aspects of non-price competition, product design, advertising, customer service and so on precisely so that they can avoid having to cut prices in order to keep their customers.

Micromarketing

Selling to small markets

Micromarketing is the marketing of products or services designed to meet the needs of a very small section of the market.

● Originally it applied to small businesses operating in **niche markets**.

● It is an effective technique for small businesses to sustain, build and grow their own brand.

● With the rise of the internet and computing it is also now used by very big businesses.

● Amazon makes use of it to recommend products to individual consumers based on their past purchases or by comparing consumers with similar histories.

● Supermarkets use loyalty card records to identify individual transactions and tailor special offers accordingly.

Marketing ethics

Ethical business

> **Marketing ethics** means applying standards of fairness and morality to marketing decisions and strategies.

Increasingly businesses are concerned to act properly and create an ethical and responsible image in the marketplace. Many will have a Corporate Social Responsibility (CSR) policy which sets out how this will be achieved.

There are several aspects to this concern…

● Entrepreneurs and managers may be becoming more aware of the need to look after their stakeholders and the wider environment.

● They may just be motivated by the desire to act responsibly.

● It makes sound commercial sense for some businesses to have an ethical and responsible image because it increases sales from concerned consumers.

● As more businesses do this it makes the ones that don't stand out.

● The internet and social networking sites mean that consumers are better informed.

● Legislation and regulations exist to make businesses behave.

Is marketing itself an ethical or worthwhile activity?

Ethics and advertising

Marketing is **good** because	Marketing is **bad** because
● It informs consumers about products they may want	● Marketing is designed to manipulate consumer behaviour
● It informs consumers about products they may not have known about	● It can encourage us to consume things that are not good for us e.g. alcohol, fast food
● It helps consumers make rational choices that will benefit them	● It can be misleading and is sometimes designed to make rational choices harder
● It helps markets operate effectively and increases consumer sovereignty	● £20 billion is spent on advertising in the UK each year. This could be better used elsewhere

Real responsibility

This is not an easy question to answer! Obviously, deliberately misleading consumers is not ethical. However, it is not so easy to do that with the Advertising Standards Authority keeping watch. But when businesses seek to improve their reputations by trumpeting positive news of their generous support for community projects, while keeping very quiet about the negative aspects of their activities, we are being misled. For example, in some developing countries multinational corporations have made small local donations to good causes, while continuing to pay very low wages to their employees. You will hear about the former but not about the latter, unless you have spotted a pressure group broadcasting its views on its web site. Some ethical decisions have more to do with image than substance.

When you think about **consumer sovereignty**, the right of the consumer to make a free choice in line with personal preferences, you may wonder how many of the choices we make are actually free. Advertising can do so much to mould our choices and preferences. Nowhere is this clearer than in the fashion business. Every so often, clothing designers bring about a change in tastes by creating new and interesting lines.

We need to distinguish between advertising which is informative or only persuasive.

The impact of advertising

These will make last year's purchases look out of date. Consumers will throw away the clothes that look dowdy, even if they are little worn, in order to look good in this year's new designs. Is the extra money we have to spend to avoid looking unfashionable worth it? Or do you feel manipulated?

Many people might feel that they have to look good at work. If only fashions changed a little more slowly, this might cost them a lot less! In thinking about this issue, it is worth distinguishing between informative and persuasive advertising. The former tells people that the product exists and explains its features. The latter is simply trying to get you to buy it, regardless of its relative value.

> *Try this*
>
> Think about the adverts you have seen recently. Identify two adverts that were primarily persuasive and two that were essentially informative, and explain how each sought to reach its target market. To what extent is advertising manipulating consumers' preferences? To what extent does this matter? Think of examples.

How does market structure affect business?

Competition and markets

Competition is usually thought to be a positive thing. It allows the market mechanism to operate more freely and allocate resources more efficiently. Competitive markets almost always benefit consumers by encouraging both **price and non-price competition**. The products they buy will be better value, either because the price is about as low as it realistically can be, or because the quality is good.

In a competitive market…

- Businesses have to compete vigorously for market share. If they cannot offer value for money, customers will buy a competing substitute.
- Prices are driven down: products offering poor value for money will not sell.
- Costs are kept to a minimum and efficiency increases: businesses have an incentive to manage well and avoid waste.
- Better quality products will be on offer and customer service will improve.
- Innovation is stimulated as businesses strive for a **competitive advantage**.
- Consumers get more choice, better service and lower prices.
- Inefficient businesses will face falling sales revenue, make losses and exit the market.

Efficiency

Competitive markets increase efficiency. The more competitive the market becomes, the greater the degree of efficiency. There are two kinds of efficiency…

> **Technical** or **productive efficiency** means that production is taking place at the minimum average cost. Every effort will be made to reduce costs by searching for the best-value inputs and organising employees so that no time is wasted.
>
> **Allocative efficiency** is achieved when resources are used to yield the maximum benefit to everyone. It is impossible to redistribute them without making someone worse off. It is associated with consumer sovereignty and with efficient markets. It means that the goods and services produced will be the ones most closely suited to consumers' needs and preferences.

In reality most markets do not reach the maximum possible efficiency. Nevertheless, by striving for efficiency, businesses do find many ways to reduce costs and prices and improve quality.

A key feature of a really competitive market is that businesses within it will have little control over prices. They can have only one pricing strategy – competitive pricing. Businesses will be **price takers** – they have to charge what the market will bear. Otherwise they will make few if any sales. Businesses producing vegetables are almost always in this position.

What prevents efficiency?

Anything that interferes with the workings of the market is described as a market imperfection. There are a number of common market imperfections:

- Barriers to entry.
- Government intervention.
- Imperfect knowledge, i.e. lack of information, either among consumers or businesses.

Barriers to competition

> **Barriers to entry** are the factors that prevent firms entering a market. Easy entry, by contrast, means that few difficulties stand in the way of a business start-up. Where there are barriers to entry, there will usually be less competition.

Richard Branson started out selling vinyl records from the boot of his car. He bought them cheaply because the major retailers had unwanted stocks and sold them at discounted prices. He was able to get started with almost no capital. Entry could not have been easier. But in most lines of business, start-up costs are high and someone has to know how they are going to finance them. The higher the start-up costs the greater the risks. The bigger the project, the more need there will be for banks' involvement and a reputation in the field. Barriers to entry include:

● The need for an established brand name and reputation.

● The presence of large well established businesses already in the market, which will be well-known to customers.

● Strong brand loyalty.

● Patents, which prevent the copying of original ideas.

● Collusion between existing firms.

● The possibility of retaliation by existing firms (e.g. price wars).

> **Collusion** happens when businesses agree with one another in order to avoid having to compete. They may agree not to cut prices, or to share different parts of the market. This is illegal but it still happens. Sometimes there is no actual agreement, but individual businesses simply avoid aggressive price cuts and don't rock the boat.

One of the purposes of **product differentiation** and **branding** is to give the product unique features that allow the business to charge more for it. This can make it possible for the business to move out of a *very* competitive market and at least to some degree, control price. The business becomes a **price maker**. This is **non-price competition**. In terms of the effect on the customer, it can be beneficial. If the customers feel that the product concerned is worth a bit extra, they get the benefit of increased choice.

Pricing strategies

> **Price takers** can charge only the going rate in the market, i.e. what all the competing businesses are charging. The price is beaten down to the point where it just covers the costs of production.
>
> **Price makers** can choose between different pricing strategies. Depending on their position in the market they may be able to raise prices, provided they can maintain the unique features of the product. They have some market power.

Large, powerful businesses that dominate their markets may try to reduce output and so drive up prices. If competition between them is weak, consumers find that they are paying higher prices for a smaller quantity of the product and they are quite definitely worse off as a result. You could see this in the market for air travel, before the no-frills airlines got started. Competition between the big airlines was weak. Air fares were high and many fewer people got to fly. During the 1980s markets were freed by reducing government regulation. This removed barriers to entry and allowed new airlines to set up in business. Output rose, perhaps by about 40%, and average prices fell dramatically over a period of years. When competition is weak, prices almost always rise.

The changing nature of markets

Information

The last twenty years or so has seen a fundamental change in the way that markets operate. Much of this is due to **technological change** and particularly the rise of the internet as a market itself.

It is now much easier to find out information about products and services than before. This increases consumer knowledge and sovereignty. Previous physical limitations on markets no longer apply: this has encouraged the build up of huge numbers of specialist retailers operating online.

Some of these businesses are very big indeed, such as Amazon. Some markets have changed out of all recognition, such as recorded music. Some businesses have been destroyed while others have adapted to the new world of e-commerce with enthusiasm.

Online retailing

Increasing use of online retailing in the UK

	2007	2012 (est.)
Internet access	33.1 million people	44.4 million people
Online shoppers	22.6 million people	34.0 million people
Online spend	£14.7 billion	£44.9 billion
Online spend per shopper per year	£653	£1,332

Source: Figures adapted from a report by Verdict Research 2008

The figures above suggest that the trend for internet retailing is increasing rapidly and will keep on doing so. This has some important implications for consumers and businesses alike.

Impact on Consumers	Impact on Businesses
Positives	**Positives**
• Greater convenience	• Small businesses can potentially reach global markets
• Greater choice	• Online sales can be added to existing sales channels
• More price transparency	• Opportunity to expand market beyond physical limits
• Access to new products and services	
Negatives	**Negatives**
• Not all consumers can or will use online retailing	• Increased competition from global online sources
• Increased risk of fraud.	• May lose share from conventional areas e.g. high street shops
	• May have to reduce prices due to greater consumer knowledge.

The Long Tail

Niche markets

The Long Tail is the term used to describe how online retailing has created a new kind of market. (Make sure you fully understand **niche markets** before reading on, see page 16.)

● Now there are no longer any physical constraints involved in retailing e.g. size of shop, number of shelves.

● Retailers can now offer all sorts of very specialist products and services to niche markets, alongside the traditional bestsellers (hits), which have a mass market.

The Long Tail

- Previously it would not have been worthwhile stocking for the niches as those products sold so infrequently.

- Now, with no storage constraints countless niche products can be offered for sale.

- The revenue from all the niches can even outweigh the revenue from the hits.

- The Internet is encouraging an enormous amount of specialised creativity for specialised interests; consumers have never had so much choice.

- "The future of business is selling less of more" – Chris Anderson author of 'The Long Tail'.

This can be shown on a diagram.

Figure 13: The Long Tail

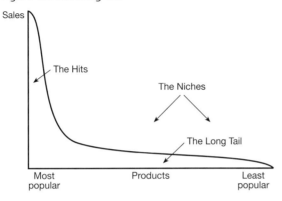

- The Long Tail refers to the shape of the curve, which could apply to any industry, from entertainment to services.

- The vertical axis is sales, the horizontal is products.

Niche marketing

Amazon is the classic example of a business that exploits the Long tail to maximum effect. Alongside the bestselling blockbusters or 'hits', it sells many other obscure or 'niche' products. In the book department at the time of writing, *Jamie Oliver's 30 minute meals* was ranked as its bestselling book. Ranked as the 1,217,575th bestselling was *Digimodernism: How New Technologies Dismantle the Postmodern and Reconfigure Our Culture*.

This means that it sells approximately 1.5 copies a year, Amazon has just over 4,000,000 books on offer, so many will sell far fewer than this! But the point is, that all these millions of 'niches', perhaps only selling 1 copy a year or less, add up to a considerable amount of revenue that may equal or overtake that revenue gained from the 'hits'. Books that sell more than 40,000 copies or more make up half of Amazon's revenue, so the rest must come from the long tail.

Try this

Think of two examples of each of the following:

- Products produced in highly competitive markets.

- Products produced in markets with one or more dominant businesses. Can small businesses compete in these markets? Give an example of a market where they can, and one where they can't.

- Products that sell in niche markets.

- Products with a single supplier.

For each product, say whether these suppliers are generally regarded as providing value for money. If you can, say why or why not.

Market structure

Analysing markets

Market structure is about how many businesses are competing in the market, and how they behave in relation to one another. Thinking about how the real world works involves looking at a whole range of factors:

- The number of businesses in the market.

- The amount and type of competition.

- The nature of the product produced.

- The degree of power each business has.

- The degree of power that consumers have.

- The extent to which the business can influence price or output.

- Profit levels.

- How businesses behave – pricing strategies and types of non-price competition.

- The extent of barriers to entry and exit.

- The impact on efficiency.

The spectrum of competition

Market structures fall into categories, according to these factors. In the diagram below, you can see what we call the **spectrum of competition**. It has **perfect competition** at one end and **pure monopoly** at the other. These are extreme situations and real world businesses are all located in the space between them.

- The closer a market is towards monopoly, the more it takes on the characteristics of a monopoly and the less competitive it becomes.

- The closer a market is towards perfect competition the more competitive it becomes and the closer it gets to the characteristics of perfect competition.

> **Perfect competition** is a model of the market situation where there are many small businesses selling the same product. All of them will be price takers.
>
> A **pure monopoly** exists when one firm has 100% of the market and no other firms exist. It is a theoretical idea and helps define the spectrum of competition.
>
> The **spectrum of competition** shows the whole range of market structures, including monopolistic competition and oligopoly. In a duopoly, there are two sellers.
>
> All market structures except for perfect competition may be lumped together under the heading **'Imperfect Competition'**.

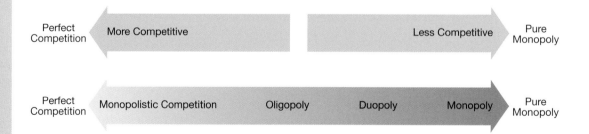

In between the two extremes you can see monopolistic competition, oligopoly and duopoly. Each market structure has a different effect on consumers and other stakeholders. These effects tend to hinge upon the monopoly power (sometimes called market power) which some businesses acquire and the consequences of this for the levels of profit they can earn.

Monopoly power

Market power

- The ability to affect price levels; either to charge higher prices, or to lower them in order to take market share away from smaller rivals.
- The ability to restrict output.
- The ability to affect outcomes in the market and dictate what happens.

And a quick word on profit...

Profit

- **Normal profit** is that level of profit needed to keep a business or resource in operation. Any less and they will exit the market. Earning normal profit means covering absolutely all the costs of production, but no more.
- **Abnormal profit** is any level of profit over and above normal profits.
- The closer the market gets to a monopoly the greater the level of abnormal profit that can be made.
- The greater the barriers to entry, the greater the level of abnormal profit that can be made.

Monopoly

Explaining monopoly

The pure monopoly, with only one firm in the market and no competition, in reality hardly ever exists. BT landlines come close in the UK. But in practical terms, one firm may well dominate an industry.

- A **legal monopoly** exists when a firm has 25% or more of a market. This means that the Competition Commission can intervene in the market if the business is thought to be acting against the public interest. (The Competition Commission is a government body that exists to ensure that businesses comply with competition law.)

- A **natural monopoly** exists when it would be wasteful to have more than one business providing a service e.g. a rail network or gas supply. (Natural monopolies have regulators, government bodies set up to ensure that they do not exploit the customer.)

- Monopolies have the ability to set either price or output levels.

- Prices tend to be higher with a monopoly.

- There are considerable barriers to entry.

- Consumer choice may be severely restricted.

- Profits will be higher than they would be in a competitive situation.

- There is a danger of **X-inefficiency** developing.

X-inefficiency – happens when there is a lack of competition in a market and the dominant firm has little or no incentive to control costs or resource use.

Duopoly – occurs where two large firms dominate the market e.g. Visa and Mastercard. It shares many of the characteristics of monopoly and oligopoly.

Oligopoly

Features of oligopoly

In an oligopoly, several large firms dominate the market and compete with each other. Supermarkets, petrol companies and high street banks are all examples of this.

- Oligopolists may have considerable monopoly power.

- Oligopolies are often characterised by **non-price competition** such as heavy branding and promotion.

- Competing on price is usually avoided as a price war can be damaging to profits.

- Although the few large firms dominate the market, there are likely to be many smaller firms, often in niche markets. For example the brewing industry is dominated by huge multinational companies such as Anheuser Busch, yet small local breweries continue to thrive.

- There is always a danger of collusion (illegally reaching an agreement to fix prices or control output at the expense of the consumer) with an oligopoly.

- High barriers to entry.

- **Abnormal profits** will be made.

> The **concentration ratio** measures the extent to which a market or industry is dominated by a few leading firms.
>
> An **oligopoly** is said to exist when the concentration ratio shows that the *biggest five* firms in the market account for more than 60% of the market.

Oligopolies may indulge in **predatory pricing**. They may try to undercut competitors that have higher costs than they do, charging prices at which the competitor cannot survive.

Monopolistic competition

Features of monopolistic competition

This is where there are many firms in the market each offering a slightly differentiated product and all competing with each other. Hairdressers, sandwich bars and plumbers are all examples of this.

- There are many firms producing similar, but not identical products and there is **product differentiation**.

- There are many producers and many consumers in the market, the concentration ratio is low and they act independently.

- Consumers are aware of both price and non-price differences among the competitors' products.

- The barriers to entry and exit, into and out of the market, are relatively low or sometimes non-existent.

- Producers have some control over prices.

- The firms may make some abnormal profit.

> ➡ **Health warning – do not confuse monopolistic behaviour with a monopoly**
>
> They are easily confused, never use monopolistic to describe any kind of monopoly behaviour. 'Monopolistic' just means that businesses have an element of market power, and this may be quite small.

Perfect competition

Features
of perfect
competition

Perfect competition is a theoretical idea; it is a model that defines the greatest possible degree of competition. It implies a market with countless buyers and sellers and identical products. In reality it almost never exists but currency trading and some commodity products come close. The following conditions must be there for it to exist.

- The product is homogenous, meaning that every supplier sells an identical product and it is impossible to tell the difference between products from different suppliers.

- There are many buyers and many sellers, none of which are big enough to influence price.

- Firms have no control over price; all are **price takers**.

- There are no **barriers to entry** or exit.

- There is **perfect knowledge**, consumers and suppliers know about everything that happens, as it happens and have full information on all aspects of the market.

- Only **normal profit** is made.

Are monopolies ever a good thing?

**Monopoly
and the
public
interest**

The table below summarises the conclusions we might draw from considering the impact of different market structures on the consumer. It shows how market characteristics are influenced by the strength of competition in the market.

More Competitive		Less Competitive
Perfect Competition		**Monopoly**
← More	**Number of firms**	Fewer →
← More intense	**Competition**	Less intense →
← Lower	**Prices**	Higher →
← Less	**Profits**	Greater →
← Less	**Market power**	Greater →
← Fewer	**Barriers to entry**	Greater →
← Less	**Monopoly power**	Greater →
← Greater	**Consumer power**	Less →
← Greater	**Consumer choice**	Less →
← Greater	**Efficiency**	Less →

Shareholders like **abnormal profit**. To the extent that they have provided finance for the business, they can get a dividend that gives them a market rate of return on the money they invested even if the business makes only **normal profit**. (This is because normal profit covers the cost of the necessary finance.) But if the business makes an abnormal profit they will be very pleased.

Abnormal profit is not good for consumers. It indicates that prices are higher than they need to be in order to ensure that production takes place. That means that consumers' real incomes are lower than they might be if all markets were competitive. This is a serious matter and it explains why most developed countries have competition laws. Consumers in the UK benefit from the protection given by UK law and also EU law.

Oligopolies have some advantages

However, big businesses can do things that small ones would find impossible. **Innovation** often requires heavy spending on capital, maybe for research or maybe for setting up production. Small businesses usually have insufficient finance to innovate on a large scale. So to some extent we rely on the dominant businesses to introduce new products and new ways of producing. New products give consumers more choices and new ways of producing can cut costs and prices.

- Where the cheapest production methods involve **economies of scale**, big producers will be able to cut costs and prices by far more than the small producers can. This may mean that the latter have to exit the market. But economies of scale can lead to higher real incomes for consumers. (Turn to pages 85-87 to revise economies of scale.)

- Small businesses usually face strong competition. Some markets are dominated by a few large businesses, but small businesses nevertheless survive quite well alongside them and do ensure that there is at least some competition in the market. Breweries have already been mentioned. Other examples include clothing retailers, manufacturers of food products, hotels and accountancy businesses.

Oligopoly and competition

Oligopoly and competition

Some oligopolies compete strongly with one another. You can see this in the supermarkets. The chains, Asda, the Co-op, Morrisons, Sainsburys and Tesco are all very big. But many of the individual supermarkets have a nearby competitor, and will label frequently bought products with a statement about how their own price compares with the competitor's. Does it matter if they all, in their way, have market power due to their size? Or are they all competing vigorously enough to ensure that we pay reasonable prices for what we want?

Contestable markets are those markets where entry is easy enough for abnormal profit to attract newcomers. However big the oligopolists in that market may be, they will be aware that if profits rise, new entrants will appear and increase competition. In these circumstances, the businesses that are already selling in that market will avoid charging very high prices. So if the market is contestable in this way, consumers are reasonably well protected from escalating prices.

- Natural monopolies avoid wasteful duplication.

- The very high levels of abnormal profit made by a monopoly or a business in an oligopoly situation are needed to fund expensive R & D (Research and Development), without which there would be no innovation e.g. the pharmaceutical companies.

- Some monopolies and some businesses that are part of an oligopoly pass on their cost savings, due to economies of scale, in the form of lower prices for the consumer.

- Contestable markets ensure that even the biggest producers will not try to raise prices excessively.

- Competition law limits the extent to which businesses with market power can raise prices.

What makes firms effective?

Managing the business

Different types of organisational structures

Individual businesses each have their own **corporate cultures**. These have a great influence on the way the business works. The culture may be embodied in business strategies, but equally it may be seen most clearly in the atmosphere that surrounds the work that goes on. Organisations are structured in differing ways. So a corporate culture is likely to find its expression in the organisation and management of the business. Leadership styles may be a key influence.

> **Corporate culture** covers all those attitudes, customs and expectations that influence the way decisions are made within the business. It may be very carefully thought out and designed to encourage innovation and creativity. Or it may be a culture that encourages adaptability and willingness to change. Corporate cultures vary from business to business.

Effective organisational structures make working relationships easier. **Communication** and order will be maintained yet the organisation will still be flexible and creative. There is no single best strategy; different approaches suit different businesses. But the wrong organisational structure will restrict the success of the business. Getting it right means considering what is most needed for success and adapting the organisation to meet its own objectives effectively. Figure 1 shows a typical, basic organisation chart for management; this could be enlarged to show all the middle managers working in each of the four departments, and the people in the next layer beneath them.

Figure 14: Organisation chart

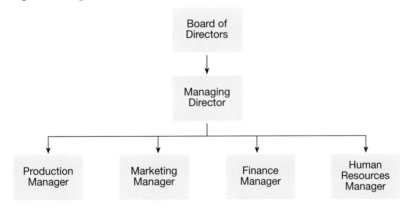

Hierarchical organisations

Hierarchies

Typically, a business will be organised in a hierarchy. Each individual will have responsibilities to others. Employees are ranked in layers. Each layer is one above the other and has fewer employees than the one below, in a typical pyramid shape. There will be a **chain of command**, so that information and decisions can be communicated from one line manager to another and so on down to the bottom layer.

> A **hierarchy** shows the layers of management in an organisation. A tall hierarchical organisation has many layers; a flat hierarchical organisation only a few.
>
> **Chain of command** – the sequence of authority down which instructions are passed in an organisation.

Figure 15: Tall organisational structure, long chain of command

Figure 16: Flat organisational structure, short chain of command

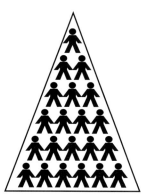

At each stage in the chain of command, one person has a number of employees directly under them, within their **span of control**. A wide span of control can create problems if the manager can't supervise all of them closely. But equally where employees are given more responsibility, close supervision may not be needed. The correct approach depends on the circumstances.

> **Span of control** – the number of subordinates directly answerable to a manager. The business might have a policy of restricting the span of control to, say, no more than ten people.

Figure 17: Narrow span of control

Figure 18: Wide span of control

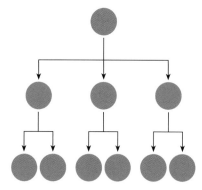
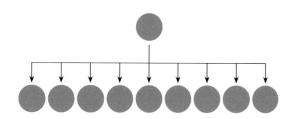

Choosing an organisational structure

Tall hierarchical organizations are sometimes associated with **autocratic leadership styles**. A flatter hierarchy may be preferred when businesses are trying to become more flexible and responsive to market changes. Or there may be pressure to cut costs, in which case it would be helpful to have fewer people on managerial salaries. Either way, **delayering** may be considered.

> **Delayering** means reducing the number of levels in an organisational hierarchy. It usually entails increasing managers' average span of control. It reshapes the structure from a tall pyramid to a much flatter shape, as in Figure 16 above.

Which is best? There is no clear answer; each organisational strategy has its merits. However, there does seem to be a trend towards flatter structures, which may be connected to the importance of good communications in present day businesses. Quick, clear decision making and willingness to listen to employees' ideas and suggestions can be key factors in the ability of the business to react nimbly to market change. But the answer depends on the type of business concerned. The crucial factor is that the activities of the business must be effectively co-ordinated in order to avoid waste.

Tall vs. flat organisations

Advantages of tall organisations	Disadvantages of tall organisations
• Narrow span of control means each employee can be closely supervised	• Freedom and responsibility of employees is restricted
• Clear lines of authority and control	• Can be bureaucratic – decision making may be slow as communications pass through each layer in turn
• Clearly defined roles and responsibilities	• Expensive, managers tend to get paid more each time they move up a layer
• Specialist managers	
• Clear promotion paths	• Interdepartmental rivalry may reduce efficiency

Advantages of flat organisations	Disadvantages of flat organisations
• Better communication between managers and workers	• Employees not strictly controlled, some may abuse this
• Better motivation as workers enjoy more responsibility	• Roles and responsibilities may become blurred
• Less bureaucracy and quicker decision making	• May limit growth.
• Reduced costs with fewer managers.	

Changing organisational structures

Other ways of organising

The increasing pace of change in dynamic markets has seen a decline in the traditional hierarchical organizational structure. But delayering is not the only way to change organisational structures. More and more businesses are considering:

● **Matrix management** means that individuals are assigned to teams according to their specialism, and work on a particular project. It greatly encourages teamwork, empowerment and creativity and gives real flexibility. This is suited to creative organisations in fast moving markets, e.g. Google. Once the project is complete employees may be moved onto a different team. This approach may be hard to manage in more stable or traditional organisations and may be linked to delayering. Team leaders have to take responsibility for managing their projects.

● **Entrepreneurial structures** are similar to a matrix system but on a smaller scale. They are best suited to small businesses with an entrepreneur at the centre. Their strengths are that they are informal and flexible.

● **Decentralising** – moving the decision making process away from a central head office and spreading it throughout the organisation, often to branch level. (This concept is closely linked with **delegation** – see below.) For example, Tesco allows its branch managers to make many decisions without needing to consult Head Office. The idea is that decisions will be taken as close as possible to where they are going to be put into effect.

Centralised vs. decentralised management

Figure 19: Centralisation and decentralisation

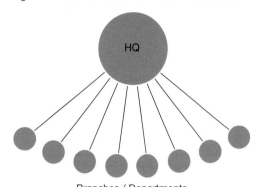

Branches / Departments

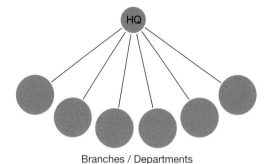

Branches / Departments

Advantages of decentralisation	Disadvantages of decentralisation
• Senior managers concentrate on the most important decisions, as the other decisions can be made further down the organisation structure	• Lack of clear accountability
	• Service may lack consistency
• Decision making is a form of empowerment which can increase motivation	• Employees may not want extra responsibility
• People lower down the chain have a greater understanding of the market and the customers. This may enable them to make more effective decisions than senior managers	
• Local managers can react faster to changes	

How can managers get the best from their staff?

Motivation

There is a range of measures that an organisation can use to motivate its employees. If successful, the motivated employee is likely to be more productive, happier and do a better job.

Many of these ideas are part of the **human relations approach**. This emphasises the importance of the ways in which people interact and how are treated. Motivation can improve when the employee feels more involved. Assuming responsibility is rewarding for many employees and produces greater commitment and loyalty. Such changes can work well if the business is moving away from a **hierarchical structure** and towards more **democratic leadership styles**. They may be important if the business needs to improve communications. You may see connections between the human relations approach and Theory Y (see page 4).

● **Delegation** means giving more individuals responsibility for making decisions, rather than having top managers handing down decisions in a hierarchical way to employees who simply carry out instructions.

● **Consultation** involves discussions with employees about working methods and practices. This creates a feeling of importance and of being valued for more than just their labour. Quite often the employee will know more about some aspects of the business than the manager. It may be particularly appropriate where teamwork is the norm.

● **Empowerment** – employee empowerment is a term used to describe ways in which employees can make independent decisions without consulting a manager. These decisions can be small or large depending upon the degree of power the company wishes to delegate to its employees.

Team working usually results in improved productivity and faster problem solving.

Raising output and enhancing quality

- **Team working** – employees are organised into teams that share decision making and responsibility. This usually results in improved productivity and faster problem solving.

- **Job enrichment** means giving employees meaningful whole tasks to do, rather than boring, repetitive fragments of work. Herzberg defined it as "Giving people the opportunity to use their ability".

- **Flexible working** is a general term for any arrangement that allows employees to have a more variable work schedule as opposed to the standard 8-hour day. It includes ideas such as flexi-time, job sharing and working from home.

- **Total Quality Management** (**TQM**) – employees are involved in quality control and take responsibility for the quality of their and their team's work. This not only helps reduce costly wastage but also reinforces employee motivation.

- **Cell production** applies to assembly line production, splitting up different processes into separate areas where teams can be responsible for one part of the process. Using team work and TQM together in this way has been shown to increase both the quantity and quality of the output.

- **Multiskilling** involves training employees so that they can undertake a range of different tasks. It improves motivation by making work less repetitive. It enhances flexibility because employees can be moved to where their skills are most needed.

Productivity and efficiency

Productivity

Production is the term given to the process of combining inputs (land, labour, capital and enterprise) in order to produce goods and services. Productivity describes how efficiently those resources are actually being used. It is most commonly measured as output per unit of input or output over time, i.e. how much one worker or machine can produce in an hour.

Production vs. Productivity

An increase in productivity will mean an increase in production but an increase in production may not always mean an increase in productivity!

> **Example**
> 10 workers in a furniture factory can make 100 kitchen units in a day; their productivity is 10 units per day per worker. If the factory employs another 5 workers production increases to 150 units per day but productivity remains the same.

Increasing productivity is something all successful businesses try to do. It means that more can be produced using the same amount of resources. Another way to look at it is that average cost is being reduced. For a business in a competitive market this brings with it a competitive advantage. It opens up opportunities to reduce prices, make quality improvements or simply increase profitability.

How productivity can be increased

Increasing productivity

- **Physical capital** means tools and machines. They enable labour to be more efficient and productive. Technology plays a big part; most modern production and distribution systems could not function without sophisticated computer systems. Improvements in technology yield improvements in productivity.

- **Human capital** refers to the skills of the workforce. Education gives important general skills and these are improved and refined by specialist training. Once qualified and employed, it is considered important to update and improve these skills. Human capital also improves with relevant experience.

- **Organising resources more efficiently** can also be important. If delays cause employees' time to be wasted, improving the way they are organised can increase productivity.

Capital and labour intensity

Labour or capital?

Businesses may use much capital equipment and little labour, or they may use mainly labour and relatively little capital. Sometimes there is a choice as to how much capital or labour to use.

- **Capital intensive** production uses large amounts of capital and relatively little labour. Generally speaking, the more advanced an economy is, the more capital intensive it becomes. Power stations generating electricity require massive investment in plant and equipment and only a few people to operate the plant.

- **Labour intensive** production uses large amounts of labour and relatively little capital. Although often associated with developing economies where labour is cheap and plentiful, it is also found in developed economies in the service sector, where machines often cannot easily replace the human input. Health care tends to be labour intensive, although it is becoming a little less so as more use is made of capital equipment such as scanners.

Markets are **dynamic** and constantly change. This presents problems for businesses and they must adapt their resources accordingly. Some examples are given below.

Capital	Labour
• Tools and machinery may become obsolete	• Skills may no longer be needed
• Failure to upgrade may mean losing competitive advantage	• Retraining is needed
• New investment in capital is needed	• In general, new investment in human capital is needed

Capital intensive production

For some businesses, it is possible for production to be either more or less capital intensive. Over time, capital equipment becomes more efficient as technologies improve. There is a common pattern whereby investing in labour-saving equipment and becoming more capital intensive will cut costs of production and increase labour productivity. It may be possible to raise wage rates and cut prices at the same time.

Figure 20: Increasing labour productivity

When many businesses become gradually more capital intensive, the supply of consumer goods increases and standards of living rise. This is an important element in **economic growth**. But it does involve **structural change** – some employees will be made redundant and will have to look for new jobs. This may be difficult if they do not have flexible skills. However, economic growth is not possible without change and as standards of living rise, so will demand for some products. Jobs open up in these areas but retraining may be needed.

Capacity utilisation

Measuring capacity utilisation

> Capacity utilisation measures what proportion of the theoretical maximum possible output is actually produced.
>
> It can be calculated by: $\dfrac{\textbf{Current output}}{\textbf{Maximum possible output}} \textbf{ x 100}$

Under-utilisation of capacity means that capital equipment is lying idle some of the time. Obviously, this is wasteful; it means that productivity is lower than it could be.

● The business is producing **less** than it actually could; its average costs are likely to **rise**. This is because the fixed costs are shared over a lower level of output.

● This means that the business is not as competitive as it could be.

Over-utilisation of capacity means that the business is trying to produce more than its capital equipment was designed for.

● This too can result in an increase in average costs as bottlenecks, breakdowns and overcrowding reduce efficiency.

● Once again this means that the business is not as competitive as it could be.

Reducing under-utilised capacity

Ways to reduce under-utilisation of capacity

● Extend the product range.

● Find new markets.

● Increase demand by promotion.

● Rent excess capacity to other businesses.

● In the long run close excess capacity e.g. sell some property or machines and make workers redundant.

Avoiding over-utilisation of capacity

Ways to improve over-utilisation of capacity

- Identify and tackle bottlenecks and shortages.

- Outsource or sub-contract some of the production to other businesses.

- In the long run invest in increased capacity.

> ### Try this
> Think about a business that you are fairly familiar with. What capacity utilisation issues does it have? During a recession it is highly likely that there is under-utilised capacity. How might this be remedied?

Clearly both under and over utilisation of capacity have their drawbacks. In an ideal world a business would like to operate at 100% capacity utilisation but in reality demand is likely to fluctuate. A level of around 90% is probably ideal. This makes use of most of the capacity but allows for unexpected orders or increases in demand.

The more flexible a business can be, the better it will cope with this problem. Using some staff who are part-time or temporary makes it easier to adjust production. This keeps **labour productivity** as high as it can be and avoids employing people who will have time on their hands, so keeping costs of production to a minimum.

Lean management

Lean production

Lean management is a general term given to any system of production that tries to minimise costs during the production process. 'Lean and mean' is an oft used expression and conveys the idea that a business that is lean is also very competitive.

Right up to the 1980s, managers in the west usually felt that achieving quality and reliability depended on a rigid approach to business management. Strict rules were dictated by top managers and they tried to ensure that employees followed them. But Japanese manufactured products had become famous for their reliability and quality of design. This had been achieved using lean production methods and a very different management style – sometimes call 'the **Japanese Way**'.

This approach originated with the car manufacturers, Toyota. In the 1950s, the company began looking for strategies which would allow it to adapt easily to changing patterns of demand. Out of this came lean production, which is made up of a number of different components. These include:

- Just-in-time (JIT)

- Kanban

- Kaizen

- Time-based management

- TQM

- Cell production

- Job enrichment and empowerment

Lean production embodied a much more flexible approach, which set out to eliminate waste and worked on the principle of **continuous improvement**. This called for every employee to be part of a team that would seek out better ways of organising the production process and sometimes, product improvements. It also required excellent communication, at every level of the business. Gradually, aspects of lean production were widely adopted in western economies.

Just-in-time

**Holding
fewer stocks**

JIT is a stock control system that does away with the need to hold large quantities of stocks or raw materials.

- Frequent deliveries of small quantities of supplies are made to the producer as and when they are needed.

- This involves building close relationships between the suppliers and the producer, to ensure that supplies do actually arrive in time and that the quality of components is totally reliable.

- This means that it is no longer necessary to hold large reserve stocks which are expensive to purchase and store.

- Average cost is reduced, which increases competitiveness.

Advantages of JIT	Disadvantages of JIT
• Reduced costs in terms of buffer stocks and handling	• Will not benefit from reduced unit costs for bulk purchases
• Less need for storage space, this can be converted to production	• If there is a break in supply production will be lost
• Greater flexibility in responding to changes in demand.	• Heavy reliance on reliability of supplier.

Kanban

**The
Japanese Way**

This is the idea that production takes place only after a customer has placed an order. Production is 'pulled' through an assembly line as the order is received. It removes the need for a stockpile of finished goods.

- Kanban goes hand-in-hand with JIT.

- It is commonly seen in places such as car factories where individually specified vehicles move down the production line.

- This means that all output will generate sales revenue and costs are once again minimised.

Kaizen

**Quality and
motivation**

Kaizen is the Japanese word for **continuous improvement**. It summarises a whole company approach to quality control.

- Everyone from top to the bottom takes it upon themselves to monitor and improve quality wherever possible.

- These improvements are small and may seem trivial but spread throughout the business they add up to a continually improving product or service.

- Customers benefit from a better quality product.

- A zero defects policy means that wastage is minimised, which reduces costs.

Other aspects of lean production include some of the ideas mentioned earlier in this section such as team working (sometimes called cell production), TQM, job enrichment and empowerment. (See pages 76-77.) These focus on the management of human resources, including ways of motivating employees and providing the impetus for continuous improvement. Some businesses will find these approaches fit well

Teamwork

with democratic leadership, which could encourage individuals to collaborate, sharing ideas and using team work to develop new products or procedures.

Time based management involves minimising product development lead times. Lead time starts from the first idea about the product, through the design and development period, to selling the final product to a consumer. The shorter this is, the more nimble the business can be, responding quickly when market demand changes. Again this reduces costs, but it does require that capital equipment is flexible enough to produce a range of products. Only then can the business redesign a product quickly in response to market forces.

Lean Production: a summary

Reducing waste

Advantages of lean production	Disadvantages of lean production
● Reduces wastage and related costs	● Does not suit all production processes
● Reduces costs of storage and handling	● Failure by one small supplier halts entire production process
● Improves quality	● Workers may dislike greater responsibility
● Fewer reject costs	● Managers may not be flexible enough
● Customers more satisfied with quality	
● Greater flexibility	
● Shorter lead times	
● More motivated staff, less staff turnover	

Lean production was developed in the manufacturing sector. But it can relate to services as well as goods. Obviously JIT and Kanban come into play in factory-based manufacturing, but the communications, motivational and organisational aspects of lean production can be applied in almost any working environment where more than a few people are employed. The use made of each aspect of lean production will be different for each and every context and much depends on the corporate culture of the business concerned. Overall, lean production contributes to competitive advantage.

Businesses big and small

This section looks at the size and shape of different kinds of business. They range from sole traders, often just one individual, up to the vast global multi-national corporations (MNCs) which employ hundreds of thousands of people and are bigger than most economies.

What makes businesses expand?

Business expansion

- **Increased sales turnover and profit** – if sales revenue is rising, output can increase and so too should profits, particularly if **economies of scale** can be gained. Most businesses exist to make profits and this is one way to increase them.

- **Increased market share** – market share is the proportion of the total sales in a market taken by one business. An increase in market share leads to increased turnover, profit and power.

- **Increased market power** – market power is about the extent to which one business can affect what happens in the market. The one with the most power is called the market leader and has some degree of control over prices and marketing strategies. Competitors may have to follow their lead.

- **Increased monopoly power** – the bigger the business is, in terms of market share and in comparison to its nearest competitors, the more likely it is to have some degree of monopoly power. This will give it some ability to influence either price or output.

- **Increased monopsony power** – the bigger the business is, in terms of market share and in comparison to its nearest competitors, the more likely it is to have some degree of monopsony power. This will give it some ability to dictate prices and terms to its suppliers, which helps to drive down input costs and increases profitability.

- **Possible advantages of economies of scale** – an economy of scale is a reduction in the average costs of production brought about by an increase in the size and scale of output. This will give the business the chance to reduce price and maintain profitability or maintain price and increase profits.

While there are some considerable advantages in being big there are also drawbacks; the same holds true for small businesses. Although we tend to think of big businesses as being common in the UK, they are in fact comparatively few in number.

> **SME** is the recognised abbreviation for Small and Medium Sized Enterprises; they are usually defined as having fewer than 250 employees. The majority of the workforce in the UK is employed by SMEs. Statistics for 2008 published by the BIS Small Business Service (SBS) Statistics Unit show that out of 4.8 million businesses in the UK, 99.9% were SMEs.

Stakeholder groups each have their own view of business growth. For the shareholders, rising profits and dividends may be the first consideration. For employees, maintaining the number of jobs and opening up promotion opportunities will be the driving factors. The management team may realise that enhanced market power could be the outcome of growth. For them, market power makes success more likely and reduces risks. Owner managers with small businesses may see things differently – personal satisfaction may be such that they prefer the business to stay about the same size.

How businesses grow

Organic or inorganic growth

In order to grow, a business needs to invest (spending now to increase profit in the future). Investment can be directed at equipment, research and development, marketing, human resources and so on. The end result should be to increase the productive capacity and/or efficiency of the business.

Growth may be organic or inorganic.

Organic growth

- The firm grows from within, using its own resources.

- It does not take over or merge with other businesses.

- Growth comes by expanding output and sales.

Inorganic growth

- The firm grows by joining with another firm. This can be done by **merger** or **takeover**.

- Inorganic growth, combined with organic growth can lead to whole industries turning into oligopolies – sometimes global in scope.

> A **merger** is the joining together of two or more firms into a single business with the approval of the shareholders and management concerned. The two firms often retain their separate identities.
>
> A **takeover** occurs when one firm makes a bid for another and secures over 50% of the shares. The firm that is taken over is swallowed up by the other one. Takeovers are also known as acquisitions.

Takeovers can be by mutual agreement; these are called 'friendly' takeovers. Or they may be fiercely resisted by the directors, managers, shareholders and perhaps also employees; these are called 'hostile' takeovers.

Ultimately it is the shareholders who decide.

Reasons for mergers and takeovers

Why merge?

The basic reason for merging is to be able to compete better. Two possible outcomes are greater efficiency and enhanced power in the market. A third possibility is that risks will be reduced, because diversification means that falling sales for any one product will have less impact on the business as a whole.

Increasing efficiency

- **Economies of scale** lead to falling average costs. This gives a business the choice between increased profitability or reducing price to gain a competitive advantage. This is relevant if one or both businesses have production facilities or departments that are too small to reap economics of scale. (See pages 85-87 for more detail on economies of scale.)

- **Sharing overheads** – one new business will not necessarily need two head offices, two distribution networks and so on, thereby saving money. This is called rationalisation. It is related to economies of scale.

Market power

After a merger or takeover, the new bigger business will have more market power, giving it more influence over pricing, output and marketing tactics. Some takeovers happen because the parent company wants to take over the market of the target company. In the interests of efficiency it may in time close down the target company's production facilities, make some employees redundant and redeploy any employees with valuable skills. That way they simply take one competitor right out of the market.

Benefits of mergers

In other cases, the parent company wants access to a market segment that on its own it cannot reach. When Unilever took over Ben and Jerry's ice cream, it was to get the customers who liked Ben and Jerry's ethical approach and preferred to avoid Unilever's other ice creams (e.g. Wall's). So they kept the brand as an independent product. In general the key objectives are:

- **Reducing competition** – reducing the number of businesses operating within the market means there will be less competition and competitive pressure.

- **Acquisition of assets, patents and brand names** – this is the easy way to get hold of lucrative brand names and assets. Nestlé paid over five times the market value of Rowntree's to get hold of the Kit Kat brand.

- **Defensive reasons** – smaller firms in an industry may join together to try and stand up to a larger market leader e.g. BA and Iberia airlines. The Co-op is now stronger, having absorbed the Somerfield supermarkets.

Merging businesses always hope that together they will be stronger than the sum of their separate parts. Together they will have **synergy**. This is often illustrated as 2 + 2 = 5, i.e. an outcome that is better than just the total of their existing sales and profits.

> **Synergy** emerges when two businesses are combined and together are able to increase efficiency and grow faster or make more profit than they could have if they had stayed separate.

Synergy can lead to a weaker business becoming stronger:

- **Complementary strengths** – some businesses have different strengths that when joined make a more complete whole, e.g. Morrison's supermarket was stronger in the North of England; it took over Safeway which was stronger in the South. The takeover increased Morrison's market share.

- **Diversification** – Businesses from different markets help to spread risk when joined together. Problems in one field will not affect the whole business. Unilever's takeovers have reduced its original reliance on washing products, and given it profitable opportunities in food and personal hygiene products.

How increasing size affects costs – economies of scale

Growth and costs

> **Economies of scale** happen when average costs (AC) fall because of an increase in the size of the business.

A reduction in AC is good because the business finds itself in a win-win situation with two choices:-

- It can keep prices where they are and gain increased profits. These can be re-invested into the business to generate more growth.

- It can drop prices and maintain profit levels but gain a competitive advantage over its rival in terms of price and increase sales.

➡ Health warning

Be very careful when using this concept. Do not say that economies of scale will lead to falling costs. They do **not**, they lead to falling **average costs**, in fact total costs will actually rise.

Economies of scale can bring competitive advantages to the business. There are many of them and they can cut costs in most areas of business activity:

Economies of scale

Technical economies

- The larger a business gets, the easier it is to make full use of specialised equipment and machinery.

- The more complex or technical a production process is the more expensive and specialised the equipment becomes. Only larger firms can afford big capital items and use them efficiently as their high cost is then spread over a larger output.

- Increasing the size of a vessel, vehicle or container reduces the average cost of the load carried. This is why oil tankers are as physically big as possible and why airlines are trying to increase the size of passenger jets. It means that transport costs can be spread across a larger quantity of the output.

Marketing economies

- When a business gets larger, advertising and marketing costs can be reduced as the fixed costs of advertising are spread over a wider target market. Also the use of costly but widespread media such as television and newspapers becomes more effective.

Managerial economies

- Bigger businesses can afford to use specialist managers with particular skills; this is the human equivalent of using specialised equipment and machinery.

Financial economies

- The larger a business gets the more likely it is to be able to take advantage of its size to negotiate better (lower) prices for inputs. Bulk buying means that average cost per unit can be reduced. (See monopsony power, page 88.)

- Bigger businesses can often secure better terms when negotiating loans and finance, because they are likely to be less risky.

Risk-bearing economies

- A bigger business is likely either to have diversified or to be supplying more than one market (and often both). This spreads risks as the business is not reliant on just one product or market.

Oil tankers are as big as possible since increased size reduces the average cost of the load carried.

Do economies of scale go on for ever?

Minimum efficient scale

The short answer is that many businesses can keep on growing for a long time and become steadily more efficient and productive. Looking at Figure 21, the downward sloping part of the average total cost curve shows the range of outputs over which economies of scale are being reaped. As the ATC curve flattens out, the business reaches the **minimum efficient scale (MES)**.

Figure 21: Economies of scale

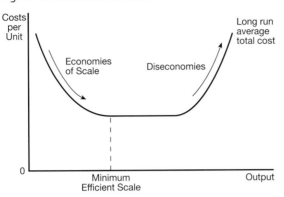

Minimum efficient scale is the lowest level of output at which costs are being minimised. For most products, there will be a range of outputs consistent with fully efficient operation. For car manufacturers, minimum efficient scale is between 1 and 2 million cars a year. For a furniture manufacturer, MES will be a lot less than that.

Diseconomies of scale

Costs may rise with output

Economies of scale do not last indefinitely:

● At the lowest point of the LRAC curve in Figure 21, average costs are minimised; this is the minimum efficient scale of output.

● This gives us the classic 'U' shaped Long Run Average Cost (LRAC) curve shown in Figure 21.

● It may be a point or cover a range of output.

● Eventually diseconomies of scale begin to appear and average costs begin to rise.

● Businesses strive to achieve MES in order to gain competitive advantage; the difficulty is knowing when they have reached it!

There will be a level of output at which further increases in size begin to increase average costs because inefficiencies set in. These are called **diseconomies of scale**. There are several possible reasons why this might happen.

● Effective **communication** becomes more difficult as the size of the organisation grows; mistakes may be made.

● Managing and co-ordinating a larger organisation becomes progressively harder as it expands.

● Flows of information can slow or be lost; employees and managers can feel remote and de-motivated.

● It may be necessary to reduce the size of the business at this point, in order to avoid sacrificing competitive advantage.

Market power

How size affects market power

Economies of scale can lead to a common pattern of development, when many businesses are exploiting the possibilities.

Economies of scale lead to falling costs and falling prices

Products become more affordable

We all have more purchasing power

A mass market develops as more people are able to afford the product

Standards of living rise

Reaching the point where almost everyone has a TV and a fridge and the vast majority also have a car, a phone and a washing machine (and maybe a computer) is obviously a good thing. The impact of economies of scale on our standards of living has been very impressive. But with this process comes a situation where many industries have just a few very big producers – usually looking like **oligopolies**.

As businesses get bigger they acquire a degree of monopoly power and perhaps also some monopsony power. This does **not** mean that they become actual monopolies or monopsonies, but that their larger size enables them to take on some of the aspects associated with them. They will have a degree of control over their markets. And this does not just apply to manufacturers – think of insurance companies, banks and supermarkets.

Monopoly power brings with it:
- The ability to influence price levels, either to charge higher prices, or to reduce them so as to take market share away from smaller rivals.

- The ability to restrict output, so driving prices up.

- The ability to affect outcomes in the market through advertising.

Monopsony power
- Tends to go hand in hand with monopoly power.

- Monopsony means that there is a dominant buyer in the market, with the power to dictate prices and terms.

- Monopsony power is often exercised when a large firm deals with a much smaller supplier; the supermarkets such as Tesco are good examples of this.

Effects of monopoly power on stakeholders

Stakeholders can be affected both positively and negatively by monopoly power. Much will depend on...

- The degree of monopoly power.

- How effective the competition is.

- The attitudes of the managers.

- Whether x-inefficiency becomes a problem. (See page 69.)

Market power and stakeholders

Stakeholder	Advantages	Disadvantages
Shareholder	• Can yield greater profits and dividends • Too much monopoly power can trigger investigation by the Competition Commission	• If x-inefficiency creeps in profits and dividends can fall
Customer	• Cost savings from economies of scale may be passed on as lower prices • High profits may be reinvested to produce new innovative products	• Lack of competition may lead to higher prices • Restricted choice • Quality may decline
Employees	• Higher sales revenue may lead to higher wages and promotion prospects • Greater security	• Terms and conditions may deteriorate if there is little competition
Competitors	• X-inefficiency may harm competitors' reputation and performance: chance to increase market share	• May be unable to compete effectively • May eventually have to leave the market
Suppliers	• Contracts to supply big companies can be lucrative.	• Contracts can be lost without warning • Prices can be forced down by monopsony power.

Monopoly and the public interest

The growth of big businesses raises difficult questions about accountability and the public interest. Economies of scale, especially in manufacturing, mean that big producers have a major role in creating mass markets. These contribute greatly to improvements in standards of living and are quite clearly in the public interest. Equally, big businesses do acquire market power and with it the ability to restrict output and push up prices. They may be able to drive small businesses out of the market by **predatory pricing** (see pages 34-35). Neither outcome is in the public interest.

> *Try this*
> Identify two businesses that appear to have market power that threatens the interests of the consumer. Contrast these with two businesses that appear to be acting in the public interest. What impact do these businesses have on each of their stakeholders?

Small is beautiful

Small business objectives

So far this section has been all about businesses that are keen to expand. But small businesses may have good reasons not to want to grow. The objective may be to make a living, not a fortune. (Look again at the things that motivate entrepreneurs, pages 2-3.)

● **Easy to set up and simple to run** – small businesses are easy to set up and run. They do not require the more complex legal structure and administration of larger ones

● **Profit satisficers** – want their business to make enough profit to keep them happy but there is no

Small business objectives

attempt to maximise profits. Profit is secondary to other motives and there is often no strong wish to grow bigger.

● **Limited market** – physical and other factors may limit the size of the business. Hairdressers or accountants are unlikely to attract customers from all over the country; they will usually cater for the needs of their local area.

● **Niche provider** – many small businesses operate in a niche market where there is simply no room to expand even if they wanted to. However, those that have embraced e-tailing may develop a national or international market that could grow considerably, depending on the size of the **niche market** concerned.

● **Greater flexibility** – for many small businesses, a source of competitive advantage is their ability to react quickly to changes in the market and to be flexible as to the product or service that they provide. Larger businesses often find this difficult.

● **Personal service** – businesses that rely on the personal touch are unlikely to be big. The very nature of providing a personal service favours small concerns over the large scale corporate approach.

● **Better internal communications/relations with staff/customers** – smaller businesses can avoid the impersonal touch. Employees know who their bosses are and can talk to them; customers do not have to deal with a faceless and uncaring machine. This leads to stronger motivation and efficiency for employees and greater customer loyalty.

● **Social enterprises** – tend to be smaller as they often deal with local or regional issues. (See Unit 1, page 3.) The aim is to cover costs, not to make a profit. So growth is only likely if it happens to fit in with the social objectives of the organisation.

● **Technology** – the rapid pace of technological change has also benefited many small businesses. As we saw in Unit 2.3.2 (pages 66-67), the internet, the rise of e-tailing and the concept of the long tail have encouraged the growth of many small businesses that can exploit these areas. It is no longer the case that businesses need to be big to reach geographically large markets.

Small businesses can flourish

In some sectors of the economy, small businesses co-exist alongside much larger organisations. Each has its own competitive advantages and customers choose the supplier they prefer. Some people deliberately choose to stay at hotels that belong to huge chains, because the standard of service will be predictable and they know in advance exactly what facilities will be available. Others deliberately choose small, family run places to stay, because they are likely to be less impersonal and have more character. They actually like the unpredictable features that they may encounter. There is room in the market for both.

Even in a manufacturing context it is possible to find small businesses in the same market as large ones. Many luxury products are sold by relatively small businesses, which deliberately maintain their exclusivity by keeping output quite low and charging a high price. Fancy patisseries do well in some neighbourhoods even though they are competing with mass market bakeries which have huge economies of scale.

Often there is a niche in the market for the small business. But this is not always so – think of accountants, who may be sole traders operating from home and making a good living despite direct competition from massive multinational accountancy firms.

Micromarketing

Small businesses can be greatly helped by micromarketing techniques. (See pages 61, 66-67.) Businesses can make direct contact with their customers through the internet. This gives them an understanding of market needs even where the customers are geographically scattered. In effect it improves communication within the market.

One of the features of perfectly competitive markets is that information is readily available both to buyers and sellers. (See page 71.) Micromarketing involves providing much more information, so making it easier for small businesses to compete effectively.

An uncertain future

The causes of uncertainty

> **Uncertainty** exists when the outcome of a particular situation is impossible to predict. Taking a decision when there is uncertainty is more than just risky, because it may be impossible to say how likely any particular outcome may be.

Uncertainty is caused by a variety of factors ranging from the everyday to the highly unusual. The causes can be roughly grouped into four main headings; the market, the economy, the government and geopolitical events.

The market

Markets are dynamic and constantly changing. Business rivals will always be trying to take away market share	• Marketing tactics; price reductions, promotions by rivals • Innovation, rivals will develop new versions or completely new products • New firms enter the market

The economy

The economy is always changing and change in macroeconomic factors will affect the trading environment	• The business cycle, fluctuations in GDP and the growth of the economy affect spending • Unemployment, affects income, confidence and spending • Inflation, makes planning difficult and can reduce international competitiveness • Exchange rates fluctuate and cause problems for exporters and importers • If interest rates change, costs may change and consumer spending may rise or fall

The government

The government exerts a great deal of control over the economy and the businesses within it	• Direct taxation can affect income and spending • Indirect taxation also affects income and spending and can also hit some businesses specifically • Government spending, many businesses rely on providing products and services to the government, cutbacks can have a real impact on some areas • Laws and regulations can restrict the freedom of a business • Trade negotiations can affect businesses • The EU can also bring in legislation that affects businesses

Geopolitical events

Events in other countries such as political turmoil or even war can affect the UK. Natural disasters such as floods or famine have an effect on some commodities. Growth in other economies (e.g. China) can affect UK businesses	• Supplies of raw materials can be disrupted • Access to markets can be controlled or even stopped • Protectionism can reduce demand • Raw materials and commodities can rise in price if production is reduced by war or natural disasters • Prices of raw materials can also be driven up by rising demand from elsewhere e.g. China

Market uncertainty comes from market forces and competition between different businesses. Macroeconomic change can be forecast but only with wide margins of error, because change is sometimes unexpected. The economic cycle creates a pattern of fluctuation but the amount of change that can be expected is always uncertain. (See pages 96-97.) Individual governments may be fairly predictable but after an election, even the changes that are expected can have unexpected consequences.

Some geopolitical events are gradual. The rapidly growing Asian countries that now account for a large proportion of world output have altered developed countries' markets significantly. The UK has already seen a good deal of manufacturing activity relocated to Asian countries. This is a gradual process, building up over several decades. It creates uncertainty even though it is gradual because it is hard to see what the eventual outcome might be.

Not all uncertainty is a problem or unwanted. Some events such as tax reductions, a rival leaving the market or a bumper harvest can bring good news to managers. But most changes benefit some businesses while causing losses for others.

Shocks

How shocks affect business and the economy

> **Shocks** are unexpected events or changes that happen suddenly and without warning. They can have a considerable effect on business and the economy.

It is difficult to plan ahead for any kind of uncertainty and shocks are a surprise by definition. Over time, economies recover from shocks but it can take several years or more for them to adjust. Examples of shocks include:

- Some Australian businesses faced huge difficulties when agricultural output **dropped** sharply following the **floods** in early 2011.

- The collapse of East European **Communist governments in 1989** and the introduction of market-based systems left many producers there unable to compete with new businesses or imports. Sales of their products fell away very quickly and unemployment soared.

- **Oil price rises:** when the rise is substantial, the increased cost of oil-based products leaves consumers with significantly less purchasing power. Consumers cut back their spending on any product they can manage without. Some businesses will face sharp falls in demand and declining sales revenue. Rising oil prices can contribute to recession.

- **A war that disrupts trade** can easily have serious repercussions. Usually, a security problem of any kind will simply make business more difficult, and make most people living in the relevant area considerably worse off. It becomes harder to sell products and make a living and harder to find enough of the products everyone needs. African countries which have experienced wars are invariably much poorer than those that have not.

- **The financial crisis** that blew up in 2007-08 was another kind of shock. The loss of confidence was so great that for a while banks would not lend to each other, let alone to small businesses. The government quickly came to the rescue with large loans for the banks but if it had not, parts of the economy might have been paralysed for some time. As it was, the long painful adjustment that followed involved a very serious recession. The economy took a long time to adjust.

- **Macroeconomic change** can happen suddenly when exchange rates change because their fluctuations can be large and timing is often quite unexpected. Businesses that import or export can get a very nasty shock if there is a large change in the exchange rate. If it is rising, exports will become dearer and imports, cheaper. Many people will switch to the cheaper import. Many businesses will find it hard to compete both in their domestic market and in export markets.

Shocks and businesses

Business flexibility

Businesses have to adapt when unexpected change affects the demand for their products. A flexible business that is used to responding to market changes will do much better than one that has relied on a steady level of demand. The appearance of competitors can have a powerful effect on an established business, but only if it is able to change the way it works. A habit of market orientation will predispose businesses to review their strategies continuously.

Government intervention usually affects a wide range of businesses, so will not usually affect competition in the domestic market unless it involves tax changes that reduce demand. Regulation can be a problem if it raises costs and makes many businesses less able to deal with competition from abroad. (But in Germany the labour market is much more regulated than in the UK, and German exporters are famously successful.)

Competition law is another matter. The authorities can prevent mergers that give a single business too much market power, and also prevent collaboration on pricing strategies. For some businesses this attempt to create a level playing field really puts a spanner in the works. (Of course, it suits consumers well.)

Why uncertainty is a problem

Business problems

Businesses usually dislike uncertainty because:

- It increases risk – the greater the uncertainty the harder it becomes for the business to manage the problem.

- It disrupts planning – a business has to plan for the future. Uncertainty makes this difficult as forecasts of costs and revenues may be inaccurate. Assumptions about the future of the market may be based on current conditions.

- It diverts resources away from the core activities of the business – managers may be devoting more time to dealing with the latest problem or crisis than improving the business' current performance.

- It can be expensive to cope with – investment may be needed to keep pace with a rival's innovation. Funds may be needed to counter an aggressive promotional campaign by a competitor.

- It is stressful – some managers may thrive on the challenge but most want a quiet and easier life!

- It reduces profitability – rising commodity prices, tax increases, investment to fend off competitors and many other events can reduce the profits of a business.

Example

At the time of writing rising commodity prices are hitting Innovia Films hard. The company, based in the UK, US and Australia, makes all kinds of wrapping for other products including cellulose which is made from wood chips. The price of wood chips in February 2011 had risen to $2,600 a tonne from $600 a tonne 18 months ago. This has significant implications for Innovia's profitability. Much will depend upon how much of the cost increase they can pass on to their customers.

The difference between risk and uncertainty

Assessing risk

The term risk is often used quite loosely. A situation is described as risky if things might go wrong. But in fact some risks are quantifiable. When you buy an insurance policy so that you can drive, the insurer has carefully calculated the probability of your having an accident, based on the information you give about age, experience and so on. This reduces the risks that the insurance company is taking very considerably. Similarly, accountants can assess the financial risks that a business is taking. Risks can be greatly reduced when businesses make sure that they are as well informed as possible about the kinds of things that might go wrong.

Uncertainty is different. It applies to situations where it is really impossible to predict accurately what may happen. Most businesses have to contend with some uncertainty. Even if a business faces very great uncertainty however, it can still prepare for the unexpected in a number of ways.

How businesses can try to reduce uncertainty

Planning ahead

Gathering information and planning for the unexpected can both help. Studying the long term trends in the market and the economy can provide indicators about what the future may hold.

Market research
- The greater the understanding of the market, the better equipped the business will be to deal with changes in the market.
- Good market research will make it easier to target consumers and become market orientated and make it harder for competitors to take market share away.
- Actions of competitors may be easier to predict.
- Trends and opportunities may be found in advance.

Contingency planning
- This means having a plan in readiness in case something happens.
- Thinking about potential problems in advance helps planning.
- If problems do happen then the business is ready and can save time and possibly expense.

Research and Development (R&D)
- If this is informed by market research then R&D can keep a business ahead of the competition.
- New ideas for products and services may be found.
- Process and technological innovation is likely.

Economic indicators

Monitoring data

- By monitoring various indicators it is possible to predict what may be happening to the economy and react accordingly.
- GDP growth figures declining and unemployment figures increasing may indicate an economic downturn.
- Rising house prices may mean an economic upturn.

These are all good ways to reduce uncertainty on a routine basis. But... it is not possible to predict everything or plan for every scenario. An airline may have plans in place for an increase in aviation fuel prices or an economic downturn but no one could have predicted the events of 9/11 or the catastrophic effect on airline travel in the aftermath, or the cloud of volcanic ash that blew over northern Europe from the volcano in Iceland in 2010.

Try this
Identify two businesses you are familiar with that might need to think about the possible uncertainties that could affect them. What specific measures would you recommend, and why?

Reducing exposure to uncertainty

Diversifying

Some businesses pursue **diversification** in order to reduce risks. Unilever has about 500 different product lines. Disaster in any one of them can have only a limited effect. Sometimes it is wise to include in the product range some **low-risk items** that can be relied on to sell steadily in almost all circumstances. It is hard to make porridge oats into a highly successful product, because generally, no supplier has a particular advantage over its competitors. This is therefore a market that is fairly close to perfect competition and only normal profits can be expected. But some people like to eat porridge so oats will sell steadily and bring in useful sales revenue that is really unlikely to fluctuate much.

Unspectacular products like this can be very useful to a business facing falling demand for its more exciting products during a recession, even if they are not actually inferior goods. (See page 58.)

Other strategies might include:

● **Collaboration** between competitors may help to cut costs. They may share production facilities or use common components so as benefit from economies of scale. This happens sometimes in the car industry.

● **Hedging** can be used by importers to reduce the risk of exchange rate changes. They can buy foreign exchange to pay for their imports in the forward markets, where you can agree the exchange rate in advance. Most importers hedge to some degree as a matter of routine.

Trading off risk against profit

Risky projects may be profitable

Risky ventures often allow businesses to make higher profits. Oil companies are always running the risk that their explorations will fail to find oil under the ground (or the sea). In return, they can usually count on getting a **high profit margin** when they do find and sell oil. Even so, they may find that the price of oil is fluctuating. They will make a lot more profit when the price is high than they do when it is low. Individual oil companies do not have a great deal of control over prices: oil is a commodity and if demand falls (e.g. in a recession), the price may fall quite sharply. Even so, over the long run, oil companies do make good profits. If they did not, some of them might in time close down because the profits were not big enough to compensate for the risks involved.

Some businesses are more risk-averse than others. Perhaps this is mainly because some people are more risk averse than others! A really risk averse person probably would not get involved in a business start-up at all. Being an entrepreneur is not for the faint-hearted.

Established businesses are generally more secure – but not always. Think of what happened to the big players in the recorded music market, when internet downloads hit the market for CDs. Or, to some airlines, when Ryanair and Easyjet appeared in their market. Could they have seen this coming?

What is the economic cycle?

The economy does not grow at the same steady rate over time. There are periods of rapid, slow, static and even negative growth. These fluctuations appear to follow a pattern which repeats itself, though not in an easily predictable way. This is the **economic cycle**.

> The **economic cycle** describes the fluctuations in the levels and rates of growth of GDP over a period of time. It is sometimes referred to as the trade or the business cycle.

It can be shown by a representative diagram. The line, Trend GDP, shows the average increase in GDP over time. Actual GDP shows the sequence of boom, downturn, recession and recovery, each lasting for a few years at a time. Despite the fluctuations caused by the cycle, the UK economy has grown steadily (on average, by about 2.2% per year). We are better off now than in any previous generation.

Trend GDP growth is based on higher productivity and new sources of natural resources. Higher productivity is achieved when investment increases, new technologies are developed and education and training improve.

Figure 22: The economic cycle

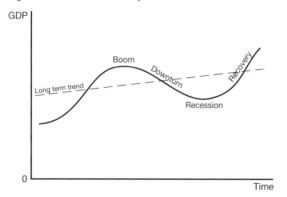

Depending on where the economy seems to be in the economic cycle, the outlook for businesses will vary markedly. The four stages are boom, downturn, recession, and recovery.

● **Boom** – a time of rapid growth and expansion in the economy.

● **Downturn** – the boom slows and the rate of growth decreases.

● **Recession** – there are at least two consecutive quarters of negative growth.

● **Recovery** – positive growth returns, slowly at first then picks up pace.

	% Growth GDP	Inflation	Unemploy-ment	Output	Incomes	Base Rate
Boom	Rapid	High	Low	High	Rising	High
Downturn	Slowing	Slowing	Increasing	Static	Static	Falling
Recession	Negative	Low	High	Falling	Falling	Low
Recovery	Increasing	Rising	Falling	Increasing	Static	Increasing

The different stages of the economic cycle have different effects on both businesses and consumers. Many businesses will do well in a boom but some will not. Some businesses will do well in a recession but many others will not. Much depends on the income elasticity of demand for the product concerned and whether the business is selling normal or inferior goods. (See page 58.)

When the economy is recovering, most businesses will be optimistic and their expectations about sales turnover and profits will make them confident. When recession bites, this confidence in the future diminishes quickly. Plans to increase output will be cut back and investment projects may be cancelled.

Business in the economic cycle

How businesses are affected by the boom period

- Sales of income elastic goods will increase significantly.
- Sales of normal goods will rise.
- Unemployment is low, consumers have more income to spend and feel more confident about the future.
- Output of normal goods will rise and investment will be increased.
- Many new business start-ups and existing ones expand.
- Sales of inferior goods will fall as consumers substitute normal goods in their place.
- Output of inferior goods will fall.
- Prices may rise as demand exceeds supply.
- Costs may also rise as some resources become scarce; this may also increase prices.
- Inflation can cause problems for a business (see next section).

How businesses are affected by the downturn period

- Sales of income elastic goods will fall.
- Sales of other goods begin to slow.
- Unemployment begins to rise and consumers feel less confident, they may reduce spending.
- Investment slows as expectations of growth diminish.
- Output slows and may fall.
- Increases in prices and costs begin to slow and they may begin to fall.
- Inflation may ease.

How businesses are affected by the recession period

- Sales of income elastic goods will fall significantly.
- Sales of normal goods will fall.
- Unemployment is high, consumers have less income to spend and feel more uncertain about the future.
- Output of normal goods will fall and investment falls.
- Many businesses will fail and existing ones will cut back output.
- Sales of inferior goods will increase as consumers buy fewer normal goods and replace them with inferior goods.
- Output of inferior goods will rise.
- Prices may fall as supply exceeds demand.
- Costs may also fall as some resources become more plentiful, this may also reduce prices.

How businesses are affected by the recovery period

- Sales of income elastic goods begin to recover.
- Sales of other goods begin to rise.
- Consumers begin to feel that the worst is over, unemployment begins to fall and they spend more.
- Investment begins to increase as confidence returns.
- Output begins to rise.
- There may be early signs of inflation as economic growth returns.

Try this
Think about the UK economy right now. Where is it in the cycle? Find some recent data for GDP growth, unemployment, inflation and interest rates. What conclusions can you draw from the data? Can you see what might happen next?

How does inflation affect us all?

Inflation is a sustained increase in the average price level of a country. It can also be seen as a fall in the value of money.

The rate of inflation is measured by the annual **percentage change** in the average level of prices. The average level of prices is calculated by recording the prices of a 'basket' of goods and services that are thought to be typical of what an average family would buy.

Some 130,000 separate price quotations are used in compiling the index, which is published each month. Any changes are converted into an index which gives the rate of inflation. Rather confusingly there are several measures of inflation. The two most commonly used measures are:

- **CPI (Consumer Price Index)**

- **RPI (Retail price index)**

The RPI includes mortgage interest payments. Thus changes in the interest rates affect the RPI. If interest rates are cut, it will reduce mortgage interest payments. The RPI will fall but not the CPI. (See page 24.)

Inflation in February 2011 was increasing, with the CPI running at 4%, twice the target rate of 2%. This was being driven mainly by rising energy, food and commodity prices. Consumers and businesses paid more for fuel, power and the weekly shopping. An increase in any of these basic costs feeds through into increased costs of production for many businesses, which in turn causes price increases. Adding to these inflationary pressures were a recent increase in VAT and some uncertainty over oil supplies due to political turmoil in some oil producing countries.

Why is inflation a problem?

A quick word about Real and Nominal values
In economics it is important to distinguish between changes in nominal and real values.

In essence anything that is described as **real**, e.g. real incomes means that the effects of inflation have been removed. Anything that is **nominal** simply means that the value is expressed in current prices, i.e. in numerical terms. Real values are sometimes said to be in **constant prices**.

Real value = Nominal value – Inflation

Suppose that in 2010 the annual income for a council worker was £20,000. A year later in 2011 it has risen to £20,500. In nominal terms it has increased by £500 (i.e. 2.5%). But that is meaningless unless inflation is taken into account. If inflation had been running at 5% then the worker would need an increase of 5% in nominal income to still buy the **same amount** of goods and services i.e. an extra £1,000. So in real terms she is worse off than she was by 2.5%.

Real value can be applied to any variable and not just income e.g. **Real GDP** and **Real interest rates**.

Inflation causes problems

Inflation makes some people better off and some worse off. It can redistribute income and also wealth (a person's total assets, including bank accounts and houses).

● Money loses its value and people lose **confidence** in money as the real value of their savings is reduced. This makes savers worse off – they will be less wealthy after a period of higher than average inflation.

● The **nominal rate of interest** may be less than the rate of inflation. In late 2010, inflation was running at 4% but the best savings accounts offered only about 2.8%. This too hurts savers, by reducing their interest payments, which are part of their income.

● Inflation makes consumers on fixed incomes lose out because their real incomes fall, e.g. some pensioners and people on benefits, if these are not raised in line with inflation.

● People who **borrow** tend to gain because over time the value of money falls, meaning that the nominal amount they repay is worth less in real terms than when they borrowed it. So borrowers tend to become more wealthy when there is inflation.

Inflation also affects businesses because it leads to **uncertainty** about the future. It can disrupt business planning. In very extreme cases inflation can get out of control, leading to the far more serious problem of hyper-inflation e.g. in Zimbabwe. This makes it seriously difficult for businesses to function at all.

● Inflation makes it harder for businesses to make accurate cash flow, cost and revenue **forecasts** because prices and costs are constantly changing. So it is very difficult to forecast future profits. Any plan to invest and expand production becomes riskier so inflation is likely to lead to lower investment.

● Inflation may make us less competitive as a nation i.e. our prices go up faster than those of our competitors. If the **exchange rate** is allowed to depreciate (i.e. gently drift downwards), it may be possible to adjust automatically to inflation, but there will still be more uncertainty.

During a boom, employers are often trying to increase output and need to take on more employees. They may try to poach employees from rival businesses. This leads to **skills shortages**. Employers may have to pay more just to keep the skilled employees they already have, and will certainly have to pay more to attract new employees if their skills are scarce.

> **Skills shortages** occur when employers want to recruit people who have scarce and valuable skills. This is particularly likely to happen in a boom or when one sector of the economy (e.g. information technology) has been growing faster than the rest. In the long run, this should lead to more training but in the short run it often leads to rising rates of pay.

Skill shortages tend to push up wage costs, and then prices will be increased to cover the extra costs. This kind of inflation can become a real problem if the economy is allowed to grow too fast during the boom phase. One way out of this is to train more people so that skill shortages become less of a problem, but this takes some time.

So if inflation is accelerating fast, the Bank of England may raise **interest rates**. This will discourage spending:

● Businesses will have to pay more when they borrow to fund investment.

● Consumers will have to pay more for personal loans and credit card borrowing.

Falling demand for investment and consumer goods will reduce economic growth and can lead to a recession, causing higher unemployment. This is another way in which inflation contributes to uncertainty.

What is unemployment and how does it affect us all?

Unemployment refers to the number of people able and willing to work but not able to find a paying job.

Unemployment does not include full-time students, the retired, children, or those not actively looking for a paying job.

Rather confusingly there are different measures of unemployment depending upon who is doing the counting and on how unemployment is defined. The claimant count and ILO defined unemployment appeared in Unit 1, see page 23. The overall figures – 1.46 million for the claimant count and 2.5 million for ILO unemployment at the end of 2010 – hide much detail.

Unemployment causes problems

- The total for ILO unemployment was 2.5 million, which was made up of 1.48 million men and 1.02 million women. Although women seemed to be faring better, unemployment amongst women employees was rising faster.

- Although the percentage of unemployed amongst the whole working population was 7.9%, the rate amongst 16 to 24 year olds was 20.3%.

- Different areas have different levels of unemployment: the highest rate was in the West Midlands (9.9%) and the lowest rate was in the South West (5.9%).

- The number of people working part-time because they could not find a full-time job reached 1.16 million, the highest ever figure.

Governments are particularly sensitive about unemployment because voters don't like it. In recent years, the number of people who are registered as disabled has increased considerably and this may have made unemployment figures look lower than they really are.

Types of unemployment

Structural unemployment happens when people have the wrong skills for the employment on offer, or are in the wrong place to take up other employment. Sometimes it can be both. It is usually associated with declining industries and structural change. Examples include mining, shipbuilding, steelworks, engineering and textiles.

Cyclical unemployment is caused by a downturn in the economic cycle. Not as much is being spent and so not as much is produced which means fewer workers are needed. A 'recession' causes the highest levels of unemployment.

Frictional unemployment is always present in the economy; it consists of people who are between jobs. Examples include graduates seeking their first jobs and people who quit their jobs to relocate or to seek out better employment. Frictional unemployment is beneficial because it means people seek out the jobs for which they are best suited, while giving companies the chance to find the best employees. Without it the economy would be static and not grow.

Regional unemployment is the rate of unemployment in different areas throughout the UK. It can be higher in some areas than others. This is often linked to declining industries and structural change. Areas can suffer from lack of investment and fall behind as well.

Seasonal unemployment occurs when there is a seasonal variation in demand and people are not employed all year round. Examples include tourism, catering and agriculture.

Costs to the economy

Unemployment imposes costs on the economy and on society.

- Unemployment can be seen as an **opportunity cost**. The alternative to unemployment is employment, which would contribute to our GDP. Unemployment therefore represents a loss of potential output, growth and income.

- Unemployment has a direct cost to our economy in terms of the benefits and financial aid that unemployed people receive. This too can be seen as an opportunity cost, because this money could have been used elsewhere, for example in health or education.

- It places another strain on our finances because at the same time the government is spending money on benefits it is receiving less by way of tax revenue. Unemployed people do not pay direct tax (such as income tax) and because they are on reduced incomes do not pay as much by way of indirect taxation (such as VAT).

- Areas of high unemployment can sometimes lead to social problems in terms of housing, education, health issues, crime, family problems and so on. These **social costs** can lead to the need for increased government intervention and spending.

- Unemployment can exert a high personal toll on the individual in terms of depression and health problems.

- The long term unemployed often need greater help in finding work again, perhaps in the form of retraining. Even if they have skills, they may lose their work habit and become discouraged.

Effects on businesses

Rising unemployment	Falling unemployment
• Fewer people in work may mean less demand for goods and services and a fall in profitability.	• More people in work should mean greater demand for businesses and increased sales and profitability.
• Businesses selling income elastic goods and services may see a bigger drop in sales as rising unemployment means less income for many people.	• Businesses selling income elastic goods and services such as exotic holidays and designer goods are likely to benefit as falling unemployment means more income for many people.
• Some businesses will benefit as consumers switch spending from higher priced goods to cheaper substitutes e.g. Aldi, Domino's Pizza etc.	• Sellers of cheaper substitutes may see sales fall as spending is switched back to higher priced goods.
• It should be easier to fill job vacancies as the pool of available labour increases.	• It may be harder to recruit workers as the pool of available labour shrinks.
• Wages may be static or even decrease, meaning lower costs.	• There is likely to be upward pressure on wages and other employment expenses, meaning higher costs.

People who lose their jobs in a recession are quite likely to find work again once the economy goes into recovery. People who have lost their jobs through structural change are more likely to have long term problems. Their skills may no longer be required. Welding may be done by robots or the goods and services they were previously producing may not be in demand any more.

Structural change has seen secondary industries such as steel-making go into decline.

Structural change

Economies change

> **Structural change** occurs when economies change over time. Patterns of demand change and we produce and consume different things. The emergence of new technologies leads to new products and new ways of producing. The make-up and nature of the businesses in our economy evolve as they adapt to both new technologies and different personal preferences.

The businesses and industries that we have today are very different from those of fifty years ago. Then secondary industries such as shipbuilding, engineering and steel-making were much more important, as were primary industries such as coal mining. Now they have mostly gone and been replaced with service, financial and high-tech businesses. This is structural change. As much as changing demand, structural change is about where and how the output is produced.

● New technologies mean that more processes are mechanised and computerised, saving on labour costs.

● Businesses outsource production to economies where labour is cheaper. Many jobs have been created in China but countries all over the world have benefited from this trend.

Structural change is not a problem if labour is mobile and can move around the country and develop the skills necessary to cope with the changes. Problems arise when there is:

● **geographical immobility of labour**, so that labour cannot move to areas where jobs are available, perhaps because of housing costs or family ties

● **occupational immobility of labour** means that unemployed people do not have the necessary skills and abilities to adapt to changing job requirements. This is called a skills mismatch.

Countries such as China are undergoing structural change on a massive scale and on a far faster timescale than the UK. It has gone from a mainly agricultural economy to a powerhouse of manufacturing, selling its exports all over the world. Since 1980 over 600 million people have been lifted out of poverty by the structural changes taking place in China. As China and other countries have become richer, they can afford to buy more exports from developed countries that have lost jobs. These countries can exploit their competitive advantage in products that require sophisticated modern technologies, high level skills and knowledge.

China's experience shows how powerful structural change can be in improving standards of living across the economy. Nevertheless some individuals do become victims of structural change due to job losses.

Implications for business

Technological change and the spread of globalisation are the driving force behind much structural change. As our economy opens up to trade with others we begin to specialise and competitive advantage becomes more important. Inevitably this means change; some will be winners and some will be losers in our economy.

There are both positive and negative implications for business. Change means both loss of markets and new opportunities elsewhere. Some businesses and professions will disappear as our economy adjusts to change and the markets reallocate resources. However it is not quite as straightforward as all this...

Some businesses shrink or close

Losers...

Although our coal mining industry was long established it could not compete on a global scale. The miner's strike of 1984 failed to halt the government's plans to privatise the National Coal Board. Many mines were then considered uneconomic and it was cheaper to bring coal all the way from sources such as Australia. By the end of that decade only a few mines were left in operation.

Coal mining was a specialised industry requiring specific skills that were not transferrable, it was also concentrated in specific areas and so the impact was deep and long lasting. It was not just the actual coal mining industry that ceased to trade, but also all the support industries that grew up alongside it and unemployment soared. The drop in incomes in the coal mining areas had an impact on local shops and businesses too, and to this day they still have problems.

Other businesses grow

And winners...

The UK pharmaceutical industry has expanded greatly in recent years; it is the world's third largest exporter of medicines and of key importance to the economy. It is a major contributor to GDP, creating a large trade surplus in pharmaceutical products. We spend more on research than any other European country, one in five of the world's biggest-selling prescription drugs were developed in the UK. GlaxoSmithKline and AstraZeneca, the world's third- and seventh-largest pharmaceutical companies, are based in the UK.

The industry is a major employer, with around 73,000 people employed directly and many more in associated businesses.

Flexibility is the key in dealing with change and the rise of the knowledge economy. Employees must be willing to retrain and take on new skills. Employers must be able to spot new trends and changes in the markets and make their organisations better able to respond quickly and adapt ahead of their rivals. The government has a role to play in providing the right education and training services for the population and in ensuring that the regulatory framework for business encourages change and innovation.

The knowledge economy

The pharmaceutical industry is a good example of what has been termed the knowledge economy. This is the idea that we now use our brains to make our living rather than our hands and manual labour.

> The **knowledge economy** is where intellectual skills, knowledge, understanding and ideas are central to economic activity and more important than physical effort.

Adapting to change

The knowledge economy is about how new technologies have helped transform the way we think and act. Globalisation and the spread of the internet have meant that knowledge and ideas flow freely around the globe. Ideas and knowledge can drive economic growth. The government has estimated that over 60% of production is created by knowledge workers.

The rise of the knowledge economy has all sorts of implications for business and the wider economy.

Businesses	The wider economy
• More emphasis on R&D (Research and Development)	• Education becomes more important
• A need to invest in new technology and communications and keep updating	• Retraining of those with non transferrable skills is necessary
• A need to adapt to rapidly changing markets	• Certain skills such as IT and science need encouraging
• Employees may need training and updating	• Investment is needed in infrastructure such as broadband and transport
• Managers will need to keep up with new developments	• IPR (Intellectual Property Rights) need to be protected
• New ideas will need protecting	• Areas of structural decline need investment and help.
• There will be more competition from both home and abroad	

Glossary of key terms in Unit 2

You will still need to know and understand the key terms and concepts from Unit 1; these are the new terms introduced in Unit 2b.

Abnormal profit – is any level of profit over and above **normal profits**.

Allocation of resources – how resources are shared out/distributed in an economic system.

Allocative efficiency – is achieved when resources are used to yield the maximum benefit to everyone. It is impossible to redistribute them without making someone worse off.

Barriers to entry – anything that prevents firms from entering a market, including start-up costs, branding, patents etc.

Boom – a time of rapid growth and expansion in the economy.

Capacity utilisation – measures what proportion of the theoretical maximum possible output is actually produced.

Capital intensive production – uses large amounts of capital and relatively little labour.

Chain of command – the sequence of authority down which instructions are passed in an organisation.

Concentration ratio – measures the extent to which a market or industry is dominated by a few leading firms. For example an oligopoly exists when the top five firms in the market account for more than 60% of the market.

Consumer sovereignty – the idea that it is consumers who, by their buying decisions, determine what goods and services are produced and how our limited resources are used.

Contingency planning – having a plan ready to deal with uncertainty and problems before they happen.

Corporate culture – covers all those attitudes, customs and expectations that influence the way decisions are made within the business.

Cyclical unemployment – is caused by a downturn in the economic cycle. Not as much is being spent and so not as much is produced which means fewer workers are needed.

Decentralising – moving the decision making from a central head office and distributing it throughout the organisation, often to branch level.

Delayering – is reducing the number of levels in an organisation's hierarchy.

Diseconomies of scale – happen when further increases in size begin to increase average costs and inefficiency increases.

Downturn – the stage of the economic cycle when the boom slows and the rate of growth of GDP decreases.

Duopoly – is where two large firms dominate the market.

Economic cycle – describes the fluctuations in the levels and rates of growth of GDP over a period of time. It is sometimes referred to as the trade or business cycle.

Economies of scale – are a reduction in average cost (AC) brought about by an increase in the size of the business.

Empowerment – is a term used to describe ways in which employees can make independent decisions without consulting a manager.

Entrepreneurial structure – is similar to a **matrix system** but on a smaller scale and best suited to small businesses with an entrepreneur at the centre.

Flexible working – a general term for any arrangement that allows employees to have a more variable work schedule.

Hierarchical organisations – in a hierarchical organisation employees are ranked in layers. Each layer is one above the other and has fewer employees than the one below.

Income elastic – when an income change causes a proportionately **bigger** change in quantity demanded.

Human capital – refers to the knowledge, experience and skills of individuals or of the workforce.

Income inelastic – when an income change causes a proportionately **smaller** change in quantity demanded.

Income elasticity of demand – measures the proportionate change in quantity demanded following a change in income.

Inferior good – a good or service that sees an increase in demand following a fall in income and a fall in demand following an increase in income.

Inorganic growth – the firm grows by joining with another firm. This can be done by **merger** or **takeover**.

Just-in-time (JIT) – is a stock control system that does away with the need to hold large quantities of stocks or raw materials.

Job enrichment – means giving employees meaningful whole tasks to do, rather than boring, repetitive fragments of work.

Kaizen – is the Japanese word for continuous improvement. It summarises a whole company approach to quality control.

Kanban – is the idea that production only takes place when a customer has placed an order. Production is 'pulled' through an assembly line. It does away with the need to hold stocks of the product.

Knowledge economy – is where intellectual skills, knowledge, understanding and ideas are central to economic activity and more important than physical effort.

Labour intensive production uses large amounts of labour and relatively little capital.

Lead time – the time taken from having an idea to selling the product to a customer.

Lean management – is a general term given to any system of production that tries to minimise costs during the production process.

Legal monopoly – exists when a firm has 25% or more of a market.

Long tail – the idea that the internet has vastly extended consumer choice, with the result that for many businesses, there is less importance placed on the 'bestsellers' and more on the huge number of 'niche' or one off sales.

Marketing ethics – means applying standards of fairness and morality to marketing decisions and strategies.

Market forces – the actions of demand and supply in setting price and quantity and determining the allocation of resources.

Marketing mix – The marketing mix is a term used to describe those tactics and strategies that a business uses to promote and sell its products or services. It can also be described as the **4 P's**… Price, Product, Promotion and Place.

Matrix management – in this organisation individuals are assigned to teams according to their specialism and work on a particular project.

Merger – is the joining together of two or more firms into a single business with the approval of the shareholders and management concerned.

Micromarketing – is the marketing of products or services designed to meet the needs of a very small section of the market.

Minimum efficient scale – the lowest point of the long run average cost (LRAC) curve where average costs are minimised and technical efficiency is achieved.

Monopoly –where there is only one firm in the market and no competition.

Monopoly power – when a business is big enough to behave like a monopoly and control price or quantity supplied and maintain barriers to entry.

Monopolistic competition – occurs where there are many firms in the market each offering a slightly differentiated product and all competing with each other.

Monopsony – occurs when there is only one buyer of a product or service.

Monopsony power – is the ability to drive down the cost of inputs because you are the only buyer, or at least a big enough business to behave like a monopsony.

Natural monopoly – exists when it would be wasteful to have more than one business providing a service because resources would be duplicated, e.g. water.

Nominal value – means that the value is expressed in numerical terms.

Normal good – any good or service whose quantity demanded rises when incomes rise and falls when incomes fall.

Normal profit – is that level of profit needed to keep a business or resource in operation. Any less and they will exit the market.

Oligopoly – is where several large firms dominate the industry and compete with each other.

Organic growth – the firm grows from within using its own resources to expand output.

Perfect competition – A highly theoretical market where competition is at its highest and purest with countless buyers and sellers and identical products.

Physical capital – means anything that can be used in the production process, such as buildings, tools and machines.

Price elastic – a price change causes a proportionately **bigger** change in quantity demanded.

Price inelastic – a price change causes a proportionately **smaller** change in quantity demanded.

Price elasticity of demand – measures the proportionate change in quantity demanded following a change in price.

Productivity – describes how efficiently resources are actually being used, usually by looking at output per unit of input.

Pure monopoly – exists when one firm has 100% of the market and no other firms exist. It is more of a theoretical idea and helps define the spectrum of competition.

Profit satisficer – a business where enough profit is made to keep the owners happy but no attempt is made to maximise profits.

Profit signalling mechanism – the means by which resources are allocated. The presence of profit in a market attracts more resources and loss sends them away.

Real value – means that the effects of inflation have been removed. Real value = Nominal value – Inflation rate.

Recession – occurs when there are at least two consecutive quarters of negative growth in GDP.

Recovery – is when positive growth of GDP increases slowly at first, then gathering pace. If it then grows faster, it may lead to a **boom**.

Regional unemployment – is the rate of unemployment in different areas throughout the UK.

Resources – include **land** – raw materials and land itself, **labour** – the human input, **capital** – anything that is used to produce something else such as tools, **enterprise** – the human spark that combines the above and produces something.

Seasonal unemployment – occurs when there is a seasonal variation in demand and people are not employed all year round.

SME – is the recognised abbreviation for Small and Medium Sized Enterprises.

Span of control – the number of subordinates directly answerable to a manager.

Spectrum of competition – a range of market structures with the two extremes of monopoly and perfect competition at each end. Somewhere in between lie all markets.

Structural change – happens when economies change over time, patterns of demand change and the make-up and nature of the businesses in our economy evolves and changes.

Structural unemployment – happens when people have the wrong skills for the employment on offer, or are in the wrong place to take up other employment.

Synergy – sometimes the combination of two businesses that have merged yields more than the expected results. Often illustrated as 2 + 2 = 5.

Takeover – when one firm makes a bid for another and secures over 50% of the shares. The firm that is taken over is swallowed up by the other one.

Team working – employees are organised into teams that share decision making and responsibility.

Technical or **productive efficiency** means that production is taking place at the minimum average cost.

Total Quality Management (**TQM**) – refers to employees being involved in quality control and taking responsibility for the quality of their and their team's work.

Uncertainty – is simply an expression used to describe anything that is unpredictable and beyond the control of the business.

X-inefficiency – happens when there is a lack of competition in a market and the dominant firm has little or no incentive to control costs or resource use. It is usually associated with monopolies.

Answers to the 'Try this' questions

These are outline answers, just to give you clues and where relevant, numerical answers. For some questions, the answers will depend on your own experience, and no standard answers can be provided. In an exam, give as much explanation as you can. Get used to providing examples of specific situations that you personally know about; these can be used to support your analysis and evaluations.

Page 8: When it became possible to download music, many people quickly shifted to this way of getting the recordings they wanted. So demand for CDs diminished. There was a new, cheap substitute on the market. The demand curve for CDs shifted to the left – fewer recordings were demanded at any given price. The income that bands could obtain from sales dropped fast. They had to look for other ways to make money, and began to offer more live concerts.

Page 12: A fall in incomes had led to the demand curve for Ford's cars to shift to the left. At the same time, consumer preferences were changing, making that shift greater. The equilibrium price fell. So long as Ford tried to charge the old prices, they were left with unsold stocks. Ford had to adapt to the change in consumer preferences by making smaller, more economical cars. So long as it continued to supply the old models, it was production rather than market oriented.

Page 19: Apple competes on innovative, user-friendly design and reliability. Its new product developments have been highly successful. Vauxhall and Premier Inns compete unashamedly on price, as does John Lewis, but there, there is heavy emphasis on value for money too. Boeing is part of a duopoly – along with Airbus. Price, quality and reliability are important but the two companies position their products in the market rather differently, hoping to increase market share by targeting particular market segments.

Page 35: A combination of competitive pricing and cost-plus pricing is most usual for business start-ups. The firm will often be small in relation to the market and will be forced to accept the going market price in order to compete. The price must cover the costs of production but the extra implied by cost-plus pricing may be limited by the prices of competing products. A few start-ups have products with unique features that might enable them to charge a premium price. Try to give examples based on your own experience.

The dairy farmer's profit in June will be TR (P x Q) – TC (TFC + TVC)

TR = 1000 x £4.50p = £4,500

TC = £1,200 + (1000 x £3.00) = £1,200 + £3,000 = £4,200

Profit = £4,500 – £4,200 = £300

If it rains a lot, total revenue after sales of 600 tubs will be £4.50 x 600 = £2700; losses will be £1500.

Page 36: Contribution goes down to £1. The breakeven point goes up to 1200 tubs. This will be achieved only if the price cut leads to much higher sales. It will probably be necessary to cut production and try to sell the left-over milk some other way. This business does not look promising unless extra effort is put into marketing so that sales rise. Winter could be even more challenging than wet months in summer.

Page 39: Clothing retailers generally expect higher profit margins than supermarkets because clothing is subject to changing fashions and therefore somewhat riskier. So M&S would look for more than the typical 5% operating profit margin that might be expected by supermarkets. Given the difficulties brought about by recession, M&S might be fairly pleased.

Page 52

Market for bread following an increase in the price of flour

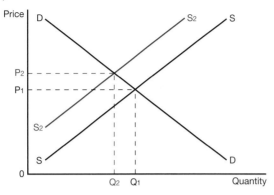

1. Flour is an essential ingredient in making bread and any increase in its price will increase the costs of production. Producers will therefore be less willing to supply as much at each and every price. This will shift the supply curve to the left and cause an increase in price from P1 to P2 and a fall in quantity from Q1 to Q2.

Market for Daz washing powder following an increase in the price of Ariel washing powder

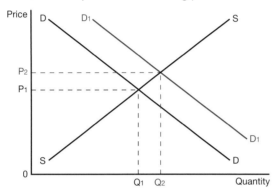

2. Daz and Ariel are to an extent substitutes. If the price of Ariel rises some consumers will substitute the now relatively cheaper Daz for their normal Ariel. More Daz is now demanded by consumers at each and every price. The demand curve shifts to the right creating a new equilibrium. Price rises from P1 to P2 and quantity increases from Q1 to Q2.

Market for foreign holidays following an increase in income tax

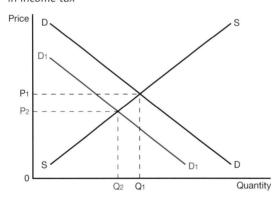

3. More income tax means less disposable income and so consumers may well cut back on luxuries such as these. Fewer foreign holidays are now demanded by consumers at each and every price. The demand curve shifts to the left creating a new equilibrium. Price falls from P1 to P2 and quantity falls from Q1 to Q2.

Market for apples following a fine autumn and a bumper harvest

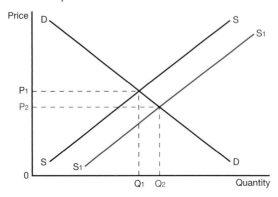

4. A natural occurrence such as a good harvest will make more apples available at each and every price. This will shift the supply curve to the right and cause a fall in price from P1 to P2 and an increase in quantity from Q1 to Q2.

Page 53: -2.5%. There was a 20% price cut, followed by a 50% increase in sales. The price cut was a good idea in that sales increased by a much higher percentage than the cut in price. However, this may mean that the supermarket is left with unsold stocks of other cheeses – the close substitutes for Wensleydale. Whether or not PED is different for shoes depends on the situation with respect to substitutes for the particular shoes in question. Cheese and shoes have many flavours and brands and PED will depend on the distinctiveness and the attractions of the flavour or the style.

Page 57: At the time, the only available substitutes for posting were phone calls and private delivery companies and both were relatively expensive, i.e. not good substitutes for most purposes. The internet was still for the future. Royal Mail still puts up prices fairly regularly and struggles to make a profit. Substitutes are now numerous, cheaper and often close – email has replaced posting to a large extent. Phone calls are cheaper, as are private sector deliveries. PED will be higher now. The realistic way to making a profit is to cut costs and increase efficiency; this has in fact been challenging for employees.

Page 58: There are many good ways to answer this question. The key ideas are market research and competing substitutes. Knowing something about PED matters because of the impact it has on sales and revenue. YED is likely to matter very much because if incomes fall, customers may switch to cheap cheddar. You can easily make a case for any pricing strategy except for predatory pricing, but the marks will be in the supporting argument. (Why does predatory pricing not work? Answer, because there are many small producers of speciality cheeses and no one producer dominates the market.)

The following answers provide examples. You may have chosen examples of your own that are just as good as these or better. Conclusions will vary depending on the type of example used.

Page 67: Vegetable producers compete strongly, as do shoe retailers. In both cases most of us will think that we get what we pay for. Prices will vary and customers will pay more for organic produce or hand-made shoes, but if we avoid paying for qualities that we don't actually want we will usually get value for money.

Boots and Superdrug dominate amongst the chemists, and independent chemists still survive. However, they are finding it increasingly difficult and many have gone out of business or merged. Their days may be numbered. In the steel industry, where ArcelorMittal dominates, small businesses have no chance at all. In contrast, accounting in the UK is dominated by companies like Deloitte and PWC, but many individual accountants flourish either alone or with a few partners.

Opinions vary as to value for money. It is hard to say whether ArcelorMittal uses its position to raise prices, because it does face some competition on international markets. Boots charges more for some products in the branches which are not close to a competitor. Smaller accountancy firms often charge less than the larger ones.

The music industry has many niche markets – people with unusual tastes. Collectors of all kinds spawn all sorts of highly specialised markets, e.g. for hand-made products. Enthusiasts will be confident of getting value for money. That is the point about niche markets, for businesses – they are often less competitive than mass markets.

Many rail journeys have single suppliers. Many commuters believe they do not get value for money. Each region has its own single water supplier and most people think they definitely do not get value for money.

Looking at the above, it is clear that the degree of competition in the marketplace does have an impact on value for money.

Page 89: Businesses with some market power include the energy companies and water suppliers. Energy companies compete by offering discounts to new customers but keep their old customers on their existing tariffs, thus reducing their real incomes. Water suppliers have had to increase prices because increasing the supply of water is genuinely costly. But it seems likely that this has kept a number of significant inefficiencies hidden. Cutting costs and prices might mean changing the way that they work, which might annoy their employees. But it could cut costs and prices and make us all better off. In both cases, shareholders seem to have benefitted from the profits.

The Co-op Bank seeks to work in the public interest and Sainsburys would certainly like us to think that they are doing the same, e.g. by being environmentally friendly. Both try to compete on reputation as well as price and quality. Some businesses, like Sainsburys, reckon that acting in the public interest is in the long run good for shareholders because it can be a profitable strategy if it helps to attract customers.

Other businesses claim that they have an obligation to their shareholders to make the best profit possible. While they should obey the law, there will be a trade-off between profit and actions that meet the needs of employees, the community and the environment. Their focus should be on shareholders. This debate will clearly continue for some time.

Index

Anforme Limited
Stocksfield Hall
Stocksfield
Northumberland
NE43 7TN

Telephone: (01661) 844000
Fax: (01661) 844111
email: info@anforme.co.uk

Visit our Website at www.anforme.com

ISBN 1905504640

9 781905 504640

Assemble together

Sixty topical
assemblies for
secondary schools

Tony Castle